YEFFE KIMBALL

is an Oklahoma Osage, a noted artist who studied at The Art Students' League and in Europe. Her paintings hang in many important collections. She has been consultant on Indian affairs and arts to the government as well as to *LIFE, THE NEW YORKER, HOLIDAY,* and other magazines.

JEAN ANDERSON

is a journalist of considerable standing who has written many articles on cooking. She was formerly with the food department of *LADIES' HOME JOURNAL* and is now Travel Service Editor of *VENTURE.*

The Art of American Indian Cooking

Yeffe Kimball and Jean Anderson

PREFACE BY DR. FREDERICK J. DOCKSTADER, DIRECTOR,
MUSEUM OF THE AMERICAN INDIAN, HEYE FOUNDATION

ILLUSTRATED BY YEFFE KIMBALL

AVON
PUBLISHERS OF
DISCUS · CAMELOT · BARD

AVON BOOKS
A division of
The Hearst Corporation
959 Eighth Avenue
New York, New York 10019

First Avon Printing, October, 1970

*Accessories in the cover photo courtesy of the
American Indian Arts Center.*

Printed in the U.S.A.

Dedicated to
the Indians of America

PREFACE

Not infrequently the term "art" is unfortunately limited in implication to the visual or performing activities of mankind. Therefore, the title of this volume is particularly pleasing, for it emphasizes the fact that food preparation need not solely be a mundane occupation undertaken as a matter of course, but can provide a challenge to one's skill, offer a test of taste, and constitute a pleasurable experiment in living.

We have ample evidence that, with the development of the more-than-just-survival cultures, discrimination sharpened to a level at which the true Indian gourmet emerged; foodstuffs, exotic innovations, methods of serving, and dinnerware for the purpose were all parts of this life.

Since it is often held that only when a given culture reaches the stage where care and thought are devoted to such niceties of life that higher civilization can be said to have arrived, it is an interesting commentary to note that the authors found foods of unusual interest in every major region of North America.

This is not the place to examine the academic problem of food origins, but certainly many of the delicacies considered in this work first developed in America and were later transmitted to the Old World through colonial trade channels. Full consideration has been given here to this provocative question of Indian gifts to contemporary cuisine. And as for the matter of early colonial survival and its dependence upon Indian foods, this story has been told far too often to warrant repetition. Rather, the qualities of Indian cooking, and the almost unlimited menu enjoyed by Amerindian consumers concerns the authors of this pioneer volume. The variety of preparation methods of these foodstuffs further serves to reveal the astonishing extent to which the Indian utilized his natural environment.

The extent to which the Indian explored and invented his food variety is elaborated in the recipes presented herein. But the ever-intriguing question of discovery—and at what price—can never be completely answered. Since many edible plants require considerable treatment to render them palatable or harmless, it is fascinating to wonder how poisonous foods, for example, were ever mastered. Indeed, what would cause a person to persist in experimenting, once he saw friends or relatives sicken and die after consuming an unknown food?

This is not a dead study of past customs, for many of the foods discussed are still regularly prepared and enjoyed by many tribes today. Perhaps this may be somewhat less true of North America than in other parts of the Western Hemisphere, where the Indian has retained more of his numbers and aboriginal culture, yet surprising pockets of native culinary practice remain in many of the United States. While it must also be recognized that many of these food practices are rapidly yielding to the supermarket, the latter are but the answer to the needs of a mass market, and it is a regrettable fact that the contemporary American can no longer enjoy the natural provender so available to his forebears.

It should be borne in mind that this is perhaps the most "American" substance one can sample today, for where it has survived at all, it remains relatively untouched in proportion to other influences on Indian culture. Moreover, this presentation of one of the primary necessities of life allows the reader to explore with delight a world usually closed to non-Indians. Although some recipes will prove more appetizing than others, this volume will enrich the palate just as the sampling of any new facet of a cultural expression widens one's horizon.

Frederick J. Dockstader

CONTENTS

The Woodsmen of the East

NOTE: Recipes for items marked by an asterisk may be found by consulting the index.

The Art of American Indian Cooking

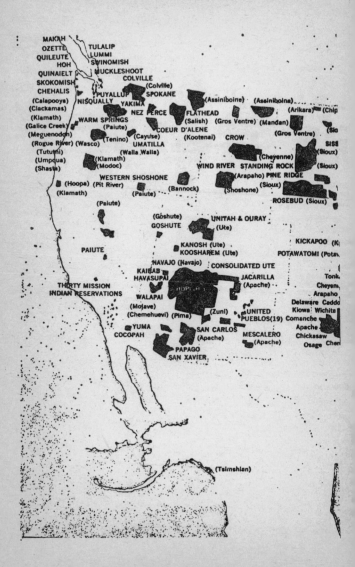

MAKAH
OZETTE
QUILEUTE
HOH
QUINAIELT
SKOKOMISH
CHEHALIS
(Calapooys)
(Clackamas)
(Klamath)
(Galice Creek)
(Meguenodon)
(Rogue River)
(Tutumi)
(Umpqua)
(Shasta)

TULALIP
LUMMI
SWINOMISH
MUCKLESHOOT
COLVILLE
(Colville)
PUYALLUP SPOKANE
NISQUALLY YAKIMA
NEZ PERCE FLATHEAD
WARM SPRINGS (Salish)
(Paiute) COEUR D'ALENE
(Tenino) (Cayuse) (Kootenai)
(Wasco) UMATILLA
(Walla Walla)
(Klamath)
(Modoc)
WESTERN SHOSHONE
(Hoopa) (Pit River)
(Klamath) (Paiute) (Bannock)

(Assiniboine) (Assiniboine)
(Arikara) (Chip
(Gros Ventre) (Mandan)
(Gros Ventre)
CROW (Sia
SISS
(Sioux)
(Cheyenne) (Sioux)
WIND RIVER STANDING ROCK
(Arapaho) PINE RIDGE
(Sioux)
(Shoshone)
ROSEBUD (Sioux)

(Paiute)
(Goshute)
GOSHUTE UNITAH & OURAY
(Ute)
KANOSH (Ute) KICKAPOO (K
KOOSHAREM (Ute) POTAWATOMI (Pota
PAIUTE
NAVAJO (Navajo)
KAIBAB CONSOLIDATED UTE Tonk.
HAVASUPAI HOPI JACARILLA Cheyen
THIRTY MISSION (Apache) Arapaho
INDIAN RESERVATIONS Delaware Caddo
WALAPAI Kiowa Wichita
(Mojave) (Pima) Comanche
(Chemehuevi) (Zuni) UNITED Apache
YUMA PUEBLOS(19) Chickasaw
COCOPAH SAN CARLOS Osage Cher
(Apache) MESCALERO
PAPAGO (Apache)
SAN XAVIER

(Tsimshian)

(Chippewa)

(Sioux)

ETON

(Chippewa)

ANKTON
(Sioux)

PONCA

POTAWATAMI

ONEIDA

MENOMINEE

(Chippewa)

(Chippewa)

(Chippewa)

TUSCARORA

(Passamaquoddy)

(Penobscot)

ONONDAGA
TONAWANDA
CATTARAUGUS
ALLEGANY

(Narragansett)

(Shinnecock)

WINNEBAGO & OMAHA

SAC & FOX

(ickapoo)

SAC & FOX

IOWA (Iowa)

PAMUNKEY
(Powhatan Confederacy)

atomi

HASKELL INSTITUTE
Kaw Ponca   Modoc
wa Otoe   Miami
e Pawnee   Ottawa
           Quapaw
           Peoria
           Seneca
           Shawnee
           Wyandotte
           Sac & Fox
           Seminole
kee Creek   Potawatomi

CHEROKEE (Cherokee)

(Sioan)

(Catawba)

CHOCTAW

(Tunica)

(Chitimacha)

(Creek)

(Coushatta)

(Houma)

SEMINOLE

INTRODUCTION

The most widely used and important foods known today are of American Indian origin. We see them in our supermarkets, we enjoy them every day, and often we even prepare them as the Indians did. Most of our classic American dishes are, in truth, American Indian—barbecue, for example, steamed lobster, spoon bread, cranberry sauce, and mincemeat pie.

The dishes are delicious; and they are all different, for Indian cooking was no more of one style than Indians were of one tribe or culture. Our continent is vast and its people were scattered. Regional weather and geographic differences determined how the various tribes lived, what they ate, and how they cooked. Dishes of the Southwest, for example, were as unrelated to those of the Eastern Woodlands as German cuisine is to French.

Five distinct areas gave us the Indian foods and recipes we use today. In the Southwest the Pueblos, Papago ("Bean People"), and Hopi grew peppers and beans which were transformed into savory chili, bean soups and salads, guacamole and barbecue sauces. Along the Northwest Coast seafood was the staple,

17

and here women of the Tlingit, Kwakiutl, Salish, and other tribes steamed, broiled and simmered the bountiful gifts of the Pacific. To the east, on the vast Plains, the nomadic Dakota and Cheyenne roasted buffalo over campfires. In the warm South the Powhatan and Cherokee had long enjoyed an impressive list of fragrant soups and rich stews, and they baked the same assortment of corn breads we know today. Two of our particular favorites, the clambake and Boston baked beans, were also staple favorites of the Narragansett and Penobscot, who, like the Iroquois and other woodsmen of the East, steamed their dinners in earthen pits. We still use their method today, calling it "fireless cooking."

The same foods the American Indian knew have become commonplace to us. Yet until the discovery of America, the rest of the world knew nothing of avocados, for example, sweet or Irish potatoes, pineapples, tomatoes, peppers, pumpkins or squashes. Corn, of course, is perhaps the greatest single Indian gift to good eating. The Vikings wrote of it first, some five hundred years before Columbus set foot on the island of San Salvador in the Bahamas. After landing just south of Cape Cod in the year 1000, Leif Ericsson spoke of "self-sown wheat fields," of "wild grapes on vines," of a land where "there were so many birds that it was scarcely possible to step between the eggs." We now know that the "wheat" of Ericsson's diaries was corn, since Europeans referred to all grains as "wheat." We know, too, that had it not been for corn, the colonization of America might well have faltered.

More than half the foods we enjoy today are America's gift to the world. In fact, they are the gift of the American Indian himself, because far from finding these foods growing wild, the Indian had to cultivate them carefully. A thousand years before Columbus the Hopi and Zuñi were harvesting large crops of luscious vegetables in Arizona and New Mexico. They had learned to hybridize corn and to fertilize the soil with guano, which they found in nearby bat caves.

Where most Indian foods originated is not known, although botanists and archaeologists now believe that they arose from the pre-Incan cultures of Peru. Almost certainly corn originated there, for the earliest known Indian motifs of maize, its stalks, ears, and tassels, were found in Peru. In addition, whole ears of corn, thousands of years old, have been discovered in ancient pre-Incan graves. From the terraced gardens of Peru, foods gradually spread northward to Mexico, where corn built both the Mayan and Aztec empires, and still farther north along the Mississippi Valley and into the American Southwest.

The miracle of corn is its utter helplessness. Because it cannot reproduce itself when broadcast as seed, each kernel must be set in the soil to grow and then carefully tended. Some scientists now believe that corn, even that known to early Indians, was actually a hybrid of two wild grasses, neither particularly productive. Where these two grasses originally grew, no one knows, although the Jemez Indians of New Mexico will show you a canelike, tasseled grass that grows in Frijoles Canyon at Bandelier and say, "From this plant we got corn." There are, of course, many other Indian legends that explain how corn came to the land. The nomadic Navajos of New Mexico and Arizona believed that a mammoth turkey hen flew across the sky one day and dropped an ear of blue corn from underneath her wing. The Iroquois tribes of New York told of a spirit woman who walked across the fields, corn and pumpkins sprouting from her footprints.

Whatever the legend, Indians everywhere hold corn sacred, a gift from the gods or beneficent spirits to be surrounded with ceremony. So great did the Zuñi of New Mexico believe its power to be, that a medicine man sprinkled a trail of meal across gates to prevent the Conquistadores from entering. The Indians' awe of corn is understandable, since for them it was the source of life. Characteristic of corn rituals was Green Corn Ceremony during which certain tribes of the South, notably the Creek, gave thanks for their plentiful harvest and beseeched the gods for continued prosperity. This joyful celebration was held each summer when the roasting ears were ripe enough to eat. Preparations lasted for weeks. Every woman swept and tidied her home. She smashed old pottery, burned old clothes, and made new ones. Finally, she put out the fire on her hearth. Men purged their bodies and souls by swallowing the "black drink," a strong emetic brewed from yaupon leaves. When every village was immaculate, and when every brave had examined his thoughts, the ceremony began with the kindling of a new fire on the altar. Then followed the most elaborate feasting. Women brought forth the corn they had roasted in the husk to make each kernel succulent and sweet. They served spit-roasted game birds and sweet yams baked in hot ashes. It was a time of rejoicing for all, the end of the harvest season and the beginning of a new year.

Such was the civilization that Conquistadores found when they marched from Florida to New Mexico, naked and barefoot, in search of gold. For eight years they wandered, eating as the Indians had taught them. They lived on persimmons, shaken from the tree when ripe; on nourishing acorn and nut breads; on hearty opossum stew and buffalo steak. It was Cabeza de Vaca, a leader of the Spanish gold seekers, who first described the buffalo, which he called "a wild hunch-backed cow." He arrived at the mouth of the Mississippi in 1528 some thirteen years before De Soto discovered it. He pushed on to climb the craggy mountains of New Mexico; he saw miles of desert and the white sands of Alamagordo where the first atomic bomb was to be exploded four hundred years later.

Zuñi Pueblo of New Mexico, the legendary Seven Cities of Cibola, yielded not the gold the Spaniards sought but the gold of corn, pollen, squash, and pumpkins that was to mean far more to struggling settlers than the most precious of metals.

Colonists soon followed the Spanish adventurers, and by 1565 they had founded on the site of an Indian village the town of Saint Augustine in Florida, America's oldest permanent settlement. From the Atlantic, they moved inland, settling along the Gulf, where they traded their own provisions of cattle, Spanish vegetables, and fruits to the Indians for their corn, squash, and pumpkins. The Creek and Seminole eagerly accepted the new Spanish foods, shared them with neighboring tribes, and the new tide of plants and animals swept through the South to the Susquehannas of Pennsylvania several jumps ahead of the white man. When William Penn was exploring the area, more than a hundred years later, he was to remark that there was scarcely an Indian plantation without a peach tree. In just the same fashion, Spanish hogs found their way north to Virginia where the Powhatans fattened them on peanuts and hung them to cure over smoldering hickory fires—the method still used today to produce the prize Virginia hams.

The coming of livestock vastly changed the Indian way of living, for it meant meat other than game. The Cherokee, Creek, and other tribes of the South learned to fatten cattle on corn to produce beef so tender and rich it could be roasted over the open fire. They took youngest lambs and suckling pigs, stuffed them with apples and nuts, and roasted them over glowing coals. That was the birth of the barbecue which soon spread north into Maryland and Pennsylvania. The Spaniards carried the idea to the Southwest. There, somewhat later, the hot Mexican moles were used for basting and thus emerged as the first barbecue sauces.

By the time the English established their first successful colony at Jamestown in Virginia, the white man was no longer a stranger to the Indian. Spaniards had entered Florida half a century earlier and traveled across the continent. The Basques had settled at Newfoundland and, as early as 1572, had sent fleets up and down the Atlantic Coast to trade food for Indian furs.

England also knew something of the Indians, for at the end of the sixteenth century Sir Walter Raleigh had tried—and failed three times—to colonize Roanoke Island in North Carolina's Pamlico Sound. John White, a member of the settlement, gave England her first clear picture of the Indians. He spoke of Croatan villages with homes made of bark and of gardens where corn was planted in neat rows with beans climbing the stalks. White mentioned, too, the Croatan way of preparing fish, of "broyling their fishe over the flame . . . they take good heed that they bee not burntt." It was also he who first described the sunflower, "a great hearbe in the forme of a Marigolde, about six foot in height" whose seeds the Indians toasted to eat out of the hand or ground into meal for making both bread and broth.

The land that greeted the Jamestown colonists some twenty-five years later was as lush as White had painted it. The Powhatan tribes of Virginia, or "people at the falls of the river" as they called themselves, were a far friendlier group, however, than the Carolina Croatans who are believed to have massacred the entire Roanoke Island colony. The Powhatans gave hundreds of bushels of corn to the English. They shared not only the fruits of their harvest and the game of their forests but also the unique recipes for preparing them.

It may come as a surprise that when the Pilgrims

landed at Plymouth, they found no Indians at all. Actually, smallpox had wiped out almost the entire Pautuxet tribe so that its villages were ghost towns and its fields abandoned. The Pilgrims settled into the Indian land and began to plant their own crops in the vacant fields. These settlers, however, were not farmers, and had it not been for Squanto, the one remaining Pautuxet, they would have died of starvation. It was Squanto who gave the Pilgrims corn and taught them to plant it the Indian way by setting four kernels in a mound of earth along with the head of a fish.

Though the first Plymouth harvest was meager, the Pilgrims set aside a day for Thanksgiving so that all might "after a more speciall manner rejoyce together." Chief Massasoit, grand sachem of the friendly neighboring Wampanoags, was invited to take part, and he arrived with ninety splendidly painted braves who then went out into the fields and forests to bring in foods for the feast. The first Thanksgiving lasted three days while the Pilgrims and Massasoit and his braves dined together on roast venison and duck, stuffed goose and turkey, wild plums and dried berries, and a wine brewed of wild grapes to wash it all down. The celebration was particularly memorable, coming as it did after a period of near starvation when, according to Governor William Bradford, a few grains of corn "were thought good as a feast."

While the English were colonizing Virginia and Massachusetts, French Jesuit priests, following in the earlier footsteps of Cartier and Champlain, were establishing missions along the St. Lawrence River among the Iroquois. Thanks to the letters of Paul Le Jeune, much is known about the land, the food, and its people. "We began to work and dig the earth," Father Le Jeune wrote, "to sow purslane and turnips and to plant lentils . . . you would be astonished to see the great number of ears of rye . . . they are longer and more grainy than the most beautiful I have seen in France." The Jesuits introduced cattle and hogs to the north country as well as pears and apples, which they believed would thrive because they had seen similar fruits growing wild.

Though fruits and vegetables grew wild over most of America, no area produced either the variety or abundance of the Pacific Northwest. When the Dane, Bering, first penetrated the coast in 1741, he found a land so rich in fish and fruits that tribes there lived in easy abundance without farming at all. In a short three months' time they were able to gather enough food to last them the rest of the year. Tribes scattered along the coast from northern California to Alaska, such as the Hupa, Salish, Kwakiutl, and Tlingit, were wealthy by Indian standards. Material possessions meant power, and they built up vast treasuries of ivory, furs, copper, and salmon. Their leisurely life nine months of the year allowed time for carving giant totems and intricate ceremonial masks, for weaving magnificent robes and blankets. Of all Indian tribes, these were the most class-conscious, even to the point of keeping slaves. These tribes were particularly proud of the Potlatch, a feast of bacchanalian proportion staged by chieftains to demonstrate their strength and wealth.

Life on the Northwest Coast, however, was not all leisure. The salmon season was hectic, so much so that fishermen worked day and night scooping up their catch in giant nets woven of vines. At other times, when their families craved a change of diet, the men went into the rain forests for deer, elk, and bear. The women devoted a great deal of time to their cooking, sometimes building up repertoires of as many as one hundred and fifty recipes. They were proud of their culinary skill but willing to give a favorite recipe to a friend—*if* she offered one in exchange! The secret ingredient of many of these recipes was juniper.

Succulent roasts, savory stews, sizzling salmon steaks often owed their distinctive flavor to the woodsy fragrance of the juniper berry.

If salmon was the wealth of the Northwest Coast, buffalo was the wealth of the Plains. The buffalo trail became the Indian trail because many tribes, particularly the nomadic Sioux, Cheyenne, and Comanche depended on the buffalo as their primary source of food, shelter, and clothing. All plainsmen were not wandering hunters, however. On the eastern fringes of the great Midwest, where the Mississippi and Missouri rivers provided fertile bottomland, the Osage, Caddo, Omaha, Wichita, and the other tribes farmed for their living. The Winnebago and Chippewa of the northern lake country were hunters, but they rarely strayed far from their supplies of wild rice. Whether farming or foraging, however, all Plains tribes lived outdoors much of the time, and they did their cooking over open campfires. Though their life was frequently one of feast or famine, when it was feast, they ate well. Rivers and streams provided trout, turtles and turtle eggs, which the Plains Indians treasured as the greatest delicacy of all. Game birds supplied both meat and eggs. When such foods were not available, the tribes were obliged to turn to the vast sweep of grasslands where they wandered, living from the land, grateful for what nature had provided.

Pueblo Indians, like the tribes of the Eastern Woodlands and the South, were primarily farmers, and they produced astonishing harvests from a land that was often arid. In the early days of their culture, they grew corn, melons, gourds, pumpkins, beans, peppers, and squash, and later, acres of carrots and orchards of peaches and apricots. With this bounty at hand, the women became particularly skilled cooks. They knew more than forty ways to prepare corn, from thickening soups and stews with corn meal to baking puddings of kernels scraped fresh from the cob. These women knew, too, the magic powers of green pawpaw juice for tenderizing meat long before we developed it commercially. They brewed fiery sauces from tomatoes and chilies and ladled them over meats as they roasted. With ground beef or lamb they stewed dried pinto beans and hot peppers into the thick soup we know as chili. They baked tomatoes with squash, pumpkins with wild onions and invented vegetable casseroles. They created southwestern cooking.

Scarcely a meal passes today when we do not enjoy American Indian foods. We think of spaghetti sauces as Italian, but it was the Indian who supplied the tomato for seasoning them. He also provided the potato that enriches our vichyssoise, the avocado we pile high with crab meat, the corn we pop, the peanuts we roast, the pumpkins we bake into spicy pies of pure velvet, the enormous, tender-meated lobster, which we consider one of the most luscious foods of all.

From the five regions of our country, American Indians have given us dishes that are varied, imaginative and indispensable. In the best classical tradition of succulent foods simply prepared and delicately enhanced, American Indian cuisine is a continental cooking that is entirely our own and uniquely North American.

THE GARDENERS AND
GATHERERS OF THE
SOUTHWEST

THE GARDENERS AND GATHERERS
OF THE SOUTHWEST

Indian cooking of the Southwest is creative, varied, and as colorful as the land that produces it. This is piñon and ponderosa country, the home of the Pueblo tribes whose villages cluster along the Rio Grande or "great river of life," as they call it. The Pueblos are peaceful farmers who labor to coax a living from their land and who have withstood dust storms, drought, and famine. Nineteen pueblos are still active today and are located to the west, north, and south of Santa Fe—Zuñi, Taos, San Ildefonso, Santo Domingo, and Jemez, to name a few.

If you visit a pueblo today, you will find life much as it was centuries ago. You will first see eaves festooned with crimson chili peppers, with strings of beans and corn hung in the sun to dry. There will be gourds and garlic, squash and onions. Second, you'll notice the *hornos*, beehive-shaped outdoor ovens where the women bake their breads. No pueblo is complete without its *hornos*, storage rooms, *metates* for grinding corn into meal, and nearby fire pits for barbecuing meat. Today, as yesterday, the women specialize in stew cookery. They take chunks of goat or lamb, brown them in oil, then let them bubble gently together in a pot with green peppers and hominy. The traditional accompaniment is golden, thick-crusted adobe bread from potato yeast, which is delightfully reminiscent of French bread. Pueblo women also have a special talent with vegetables, of baking carrots whole so that the flavor is faintly caramel, or toasting sweet peppers over the fire so that their bitter skins blacken and slake off leaving the flesh mellow, of simmering squash and squash blossoms into a delicate stew.

Like the Pueblos, the Hopi, who are known as "the peaceful of all people," grow twelve varieties of beans that range in color from black to white and include the large, flat, multicolored Hopi bean that is believed to be the original North American bean. They also grow four kinds of corn—white, which is the main crop; yellow, blue, and red. The Hopi woman uses discriminatingly the meal of each one to produce different flavor effects. The white is ground for gruel and breads, the sweeter yellow is roasted and eaten off the tender young cob; the rarer red and blue are usually reserved for the feathery piki bread, which is as light and crisply layered as the finest French *vol au vent*. Hopi girls are taught early the art of bread baking. They must learn to bake in the outdoor oven, to grind meal on a *metate*, to prepare the ceremonial *chukuviki*, which are small pointed loaves steamed in corn-husk wrappers. But most important, a Hopi girl must become skilled and quick at the piki stone, for the Hopi believe that until girls can make piki, they are not ready for marriage. Even today, this fragile, pastel-colored pastry can be made only on a piki stone.

Hopi and Pueblo boys learn early, too, how to sow, weed, and harvest crops. In the past they planted prayer sticks by the "great river" each spring and beseeched the gods for prosperity. If their prayers were not answered, the Pueblos and Hopi turned to gathering piñon nuts and acorns, wild roots, grasses, and seeds. Regardless of where it came from, all food was

30

accepted with thanks and reverence. "What the land grows and gives forth is for everyone," the Indians believe, and they are careful to divide food evenly. Meals are always eaten from communal bowls, so that each guest or family member may eat as much as he wants.

Among all tribes, each meal was, and still is, preceded by prayer. Although the words differ somewhat from tribe to tribe, the universal spirit of reverence and giving of thanks are reflected in the Zuñi ritual. At a barbecue, for example, when all persons are gathered, they select small bits of meat, blow upon them, then repeat together:

"Receive! Oh, souls of my ancestry, and eat; resuscitate, by means of your wondrous knowledge, your hearts; return unto us of yours the water we need, of yours the seeds of the earth, of yours the meaning of attaining great age."

As the last words are repeated, the small pieces are cast into the fire. Then the great meal begins.

At meals in the old Southwest there might be squash blossoms, plucked from the vine and fried to a golden crispness; piñon soup, lighter and more delicate than the finest vichyssoise; succulent braised lamb shanks; or that favorite with all Pueblos, green chili stew served up with oven-fresh slices of adobe bread and a crisp salad of marinated cucumbers. If you visit the Southwest today, you'll find many of these same dishes on the menu. You can also create them in your own kitchen. They're all here, and they're all as easy to prepare as they are to eat.

Squash blossoms are considered the greatest of delicacies by the Zuñi. Choicest of all are the largest male flowers, which are carefully gathered from the vine, fried in deep fat, and served as an appetizer or used as a seasoning for vegetables, soups, and stews.

BATTER-FRIED SQUASH BLOSSOMS

(A hot hors d'oeuvre for 8 persons)

> 3 dozen squash blossoms, picked as they are just
>   about to open. (Try to get as many male blossoms
>   as possible; they are larger.)
> 1 cup milk
> 1 tablespoon flour
> 1 teaspoon salt
> ⅛ teaspoon fresh ground pepper
> ½ cup cooking oil
> Paprika (garnish)

1. In a shaker jar, combine milk, flour, salt, and pepper.

2. Place squash blossoms in a large pie tin and gently pour the milk-flour mixture over them.

3. Heat the oil in a large heavy skillet until a drop of water will sizzle. Fry the batter-coated blossoms in the hot oil until golden brown. Drain on paper toweling and sprinkle with paprika. Serve hot.

WESTERN CHILI DIP

(Makes about 2½ Cups)

> 3 strips bacon, cut crosswise into julienne strips
> 2 medium yellow onions, peeled and minced
> 3 small hot green chili peppers, minced
> 2 cups canned tomatoes with basil
> ½ teaspoon cumin seed, crushed
> 1 teaspoon sugar
> 1 teaspoon salt
> 1 clove garlic, peeled and crushed
> Juice of ½ lemon
> 2 dashes Tabasco
> 1 cup grated sharp Cheddar cheese

1. Brown the bacon in a large heavy skillet.

2. Add the onions and sauté slowly until golden.

3. Mix in the peppers and tomatoes, and simmer, stirring, for 15 minutes.

4. Remove from heat and stir in remaining ingredients. Garnish, if you like, with a little grated Cheddar cheese. Serve as a dip for corn or potato chips or crackers.

The *piñon* is probably the most important tree in the Southwest to the Indians living there. Its logs provide heat, and in winter the air everywhere is fragrant with the scent of piñon fires. The fruit of the tree, piñon or pine nuts, are highly prized for their smooth texture and delicate evergreen flavor. Pueblo women toss them into appetizers, soups, and salads. They toast the whole nuts slowly for eating out of the hand or pound the raw nuts into a paste with which they make flat fried cakes.

FRESH ROASTED PIÑON NUTS

(Makes 1 Pound)

1 pound raw shelled piñon nuts

Spread the nuts in a large shallow baking pan and roast in a slow oven, 300° F., for 1 hour, stirring frequently so that the nuts become evenly browned. You will not have to add any butter or oil—the nuts themselves are very oily. Serve as you would roasted peanuts.

AVOCADO AND PIÑON NUT APPETIZER

(Makes 4 Servings)

2 ripe avocados
Juice of 1 lemon
Juice of 1 lime (or ½ orange)
½ cup chopped piñon nuts
*1 firm tomato, cored, cubed, and drained on paper
    toweling*
3 scallions, sliced thin (include tops)
½ clove garlic, peeled and crushed
¼ teaspoon crushed coriander seed
¼ teaspoon fresh ground pepper
1 teaspoon Worcestershire sauce
¼ teaspoon Tabasco sauce
¼ teaspoon salt
Pimiento slivers (garnish)
Parsley or water cress sprigs (garnish)

1. Halve avocados, remove seeds; scoop out flesh and mix with lemon and lime juices. Put through a food mill or purée in a blender.

2. Mix in all remaining ingredients except the garnishes.

3. Fill the four avocado shells. Garnish with pimiento slivers and sprigs of parsley or water cress. Serve as an appetizer or salad.

GUACAMOLE

(Makes about 3 Cups)

> 2 ripe avocados
> Juice of 1½ lemons
> 1 onion, peeled and minced
> ½ clove garlic, peeled and crushed
> 1 teaspoon crushed red chilies
> ¼ teaspoon salt
> 1 teaspoon Worcestershire sauce
> 1 small, firm tomato, cubed (leave the skin on)

1. Scoop the flesh from the avocados and mash with a fork in the lemon juice.

2. Mix in remaining ingredients.

3. Chill well and serve as a dip for corn chips.

Soups

BLACK BEAN SOUP

(Makes 6 Servings)

> 1 cup sliced leeks
> ⅓ cup oil
> 2 cloves garlic, peeled and crushed
> 2 (1 lb.) cans black beans
> ½ cup water
> 1 teaspoon salt
> ⅛ teaspoon fresh ground pepper

1. Sauté the leeks in the oil in a large saucepan until golden. Add the garlic and 1 can of beans with their liquid. Mash up the beans with a fork.

2. Add the second can of beans with their liquid, but do not mash. Stir in the water, salt, and pepper, and simmer, covered, for 40 minutes, stirring occasionally. Serve hot.

LIMA BEAN AND TOMATO SOUP

(Makes 6 Servings)

> 1 (1 lb.) package dried Lima beans
> 3 quarts water
> 1 sprig parsley
> 2 yellow onions, peeled and sliced
> ¼ pound salt pork
> 3 tomatoes, washed and cored
> 1 chili pequin, crushed
> 1 tablespoon salt

1. Soak the beans in 1½ quarts water for 3½ hours. Drain and rinse.

2. Place in a large heavy kettle, cover with 1½ quarts water, add remaining ingredients, and simmer slowly, covered, for 1 hour. Uncover and simmer for 1 hour longer. Serve hot.

PEPPERY POTATO-TOMATO SOUP

(Makes 8–10 Servings)

6 tomatoes, washed and cored
8 medium potatoes, washed and peeled
2 yellow onions, peeled and sliced
1 quart water
½ small red chili pepper, crushed
1 green pepper, washed and sliced (include seeds)
1 sprig parsley
1 tablespoon salt

1. Place the tomatoes, potatoes, onions, and water in a large, heavy kettle. Simmer for about 1 hour or until the potatoes are tender.

2. Break up the potatoes with a fork into bite-sized pieces, mash the tomatoes slightly, then add remaining ingredients and simmer for 20 to 25 minutes or until the peppers are tender. Serve hot.

PIÑON SOUP

(Makes 8–10 Servings)

> 1 pound raw piñon nuts
> 1 quart milk
> 2 cups water
> 5 scallions, sliced
> 2 coriander seeds
> 2 dried mint leaves
> 2 (5.4 gram) envelopes instant chicken broth
> ¼ teaspoon pepper
> Minced chives to garnish

1. Heat together all ingredients except chives in a saucepan until mixture simmers. Then simmer, stirring occasionally, for 20 to 25 minutes.

2. Purée mixture in a blender until smooth. Reheat and serve garnished with minced chives. Or chill and serve iced. Make the portions small; the soup is rich!

PINTO BEAN SPOON SOUP

(Makes 6 Servings)

> 1 pound dry pinto beans or red kidney beans
> 3½ quarts water
> 1 lamb shank, cracked
> 1 Bermuda onion, peeled and quartered
> 1 clove garlic, peeled and crushed
> 4 peppercorns
> 1 tablespoon salt

Place all ingredients in a large, heavy kettle and simmer slowly, stirring occasionally, for about 4 hours or until the lamb falls from the bone. Remove bone and serve.

Coriander, a pungent herb that belongs to the carrot family, was introduced to the Indians of the Southwest long ago by the Mexicans. Today it is cultivated by Zuñi women, who use its leaves as a salad, its seeds as a seasoning for meat and chili.

BEEF BALLS IN SAFFRON BROTH

(Makes 6–8 Servings)

BEEF BALLS:

1½ pounds ground chuck
½ cup corn meal
1 onion, peeled and minced
2 cloves garlic, peeled and crushed
1 egg
2 teaspoons salt
¼ teaspoon fresh ground pepper
1 teaspoon crushed coriander seed

SAFFRON BALLS:

4 tablespoons butter or margarine
4 tablespoons flour
6 cups water
10 dried mint leaves
½ teaspoon saffron mixed with 1 tablespoon warm water
2 teaspoons salt
6 peppercorns

1. Mix together all beef-ball ingredients and shape into small balls about the size of walnuts. These can be made ahead and refrigerated until time to use.

2. For the broth, melt the butter or margarine and brown the flour in it. Add the water, stirring rapidly. Add remaining ingredients and bring mixture to a boil.

3. Drop in beef balls and simmer about 15 to 20 minutes. Serve hot.

NUT AND MINT SOUP

(Makes 6–8 Servings)

> 2 (10½ oz.) cans beef consommé
> 3 cups water
> ½ cup raw piñon nuts
> 2 (1 lb. 4 oz.) cans chick-peas, drained and rinsed
> Leaves of 2 stalks mint, washed

1. Place the consommé, water, and piñon nuts in a large saucepan and bring to a boil.

2. Reduce heat, add chick-peas, and simmer 15 minutes.

3. Turn heat off, add mint leaves, and let steep about a minute. Serve at once, seasoning each helping with fresh ground pepper.

Main Dishes

PEPPERY TRIPE STEW

(Makes 6–8 Servings)

> 2 pounds tripe cut into pieces about 1″ × 2″
> 2 gallons water
> 1 tablespoon salt
> 1 cup sliced scallions
> ½ hot red chili pepper, pounded (use a whole
>   pepper if you like hot dishes)

2 green peppers, washed and sliced (include seeds)
⅓ cup minced parsley
¼ pound mushrooms, wiped and sliced
2 tomatoes, washed and halved

1. Cover the tripe with a gallon of water and bring to a boil. Meanwhile, mix the second gallon of water with the salt and bring to a boil. Drain the tripe and cover with the salty water. Boil slowly for 2 hours.

2. Add the scallions, hot red chili pepper, green peppers, and parsley. Simmer gently for 1½ hours.

3. Stir in the mushrooms and tomatoes and simmer for about 45 minutes longer. Serve piping hot as a main dish.

LAMB-STUFFED SWEET RED PEPPERS

(Makes 6 Servings)

6 firm, large sweet red peppers
1½ pounds ground lamb
1 tablespoon butter or margarine
½ cup chopped onions
1½ cups coarsely chopped mushrooms
1½ teaspoons salt
½ teaspoon powdered savory
½ teaspoon marjoram
¼ teaspoon fresh ground pepper
1 clove garlic, peeled and crushed
3 ripe tomatoes, washed, cored and coarsely chopped
1 cup prepared poultry stuffing

1. Wash peppers well, core, remove seeds, and drain upside down on paper toweling.

2. Brown the lamb in the butter or margarine in a large, heavy skillet. Add onions and mushrooms, and sauté until onions are golden brown. Add remaining

ingredients, and simmer, stirring occasionally, for 45 minutes. Cool mixture to room temperature.

3. Fill the peppers with the meat mixture, heaping it up. Place peppers in a baking pan and bake in a moderate oven, 350° F., for 1½ hours.

TAMALES

(Makes about 50)

HUSKS:

50 large dried corn husks

MEAT FILLING:

1⅓ pounds cooked boned chicken, chopped
⅔ pound cooked boned pork loin, chopped
3 cloves garlic, peeled and crushed
1 cup shortening
¾ cup chicken stock or broth (or chicken and pork stock mixed)
3 tablespoons chili powder
1¼ teaspoons cumin powder
⅛ teaspoon fresh ground black pepper
½ cup prepared chili sauce
1 teaspoon Tabasco sauce
1 hot red chili pepper, crushed
2 teaspoons salt

MASA:

4 cups masa harina*
½ cup shortening
1 teaspoon salt
3 cups chicken stock or broth

1. Cover the dried husks with boiling water and soak for 2 hours.

* This is a special, flourlike mixture used for making tamales and tortillas. You can buy it in specialty food shops or in Spanish groceries.

2. Brown the garlic, chickens, and pork in the shortening. Make a paste of the chicken stock, chili powder, cumin powder, and fresh ground black pepper, and stir into the meat.

3. Add the remaining filling ingredients, and simmer gently, stirring occasionally, for about 45 minutes. Taste the mixture for seasoning. If you like hotter tamales, add an additional ½ teaspoon Tabasco.

4. For the masa spread, mix the masa harina, shortening, salt, and stock together well with your hands.

5. To roll the tamales, spread a husk as flat as possible, place 1 tablespoon of the masa mixture in the center, and spread downward, leaving margins of an inch and a half at the sides and bottom. Top with 1 tablespoon of the meat filling and spread over the masa but not quite to the edges of it.

6. Fold the bottom margin of husk over the masa and meat filling, then fold the right and left sides in. Leave the top open. Repeat until all tamales have been rolled.

7. Stand the tamales, sealed end down, in the center of a large steamer. Fill in the outside with additional husks or crumpled aluminum foil so that the tamales will stand by themselves.

8. Fill the bottom of the steamer with water, then steam the tamales, covered, for 2½ hours. Serve hot or cold. Any leftover tamales can be resteamed for about 30 minutes and then eaten hot.

Hominy or "corn without skin," as the Indians called it, is a staple among the Zuñi, who simmer it for hours with lamb and green peppers to produce a savory and succulent stew. Giant kettles of green chili stew are prepared for the various ceremonial feasts. And some Pueblos keep a pot of it bubbling to offer friends and strangers who come to visit.

ZUÑI GREEN CHILI STEW

(Makes 12–14 Servings)

> *3 pounds boned lamb cut into 1½" cubes*
> *Flour for dusting*
> *2 tablespoons cooking oil*
> *¼ teaspoon fresh ground black pepper*
> *6 dried juniper berries, crushed*
> *2 yellow onions, peeled and chopped*
> *5½ cups canned hominy (include liquid)*
> *1 medium-sized dried hot red chili pepper, crushed*
> *1 tablespoon salt*
> *2 cloves garlic, peeled and crushed*
> *2 teaspoons orégano*
> *½ cup minced fresh parsley*
> *6 green peppers, washed, cored and quartered*
>   *(include some seeds)*
> *1 quart water*

1. Dust lamb cubes lightly with flour.

2. Brown lamb slowly on all sides in the cooking oil in a large heavy kettle. As the meat browns, add the black pepper and crushed juniper berries.

3. Transfer meat to paper toweling to drain. In the same kettle, sauté the onions slowly until golden. Return meat to kettle.

4. Mix in the remaining ingredients, cover, and simmer for 1½ hours, stirring occasionally.

BARBECUED PORK ROAST

(Makes 6–8 Servings)

1 (5½ lb.) rib roast of pork

BARBECUE SAUCE:

½ cup cooking oil
3 yellow onions, peeled and minced
4 cloves garlic, peeled and crushed
6 dried juniper berries, crushed
½ teaspoon crushed coriander seed
1 bay leaf, crumbled
2 pounds ripe tomatoes, washed and quartered
1 cup cider vinegar
1 cup water
1 red chili pepper, crushed
2 teaspoons salt
1 tablespoon chili powder
1 square unsweetened chocolate, grated

1. Heat the oil in a large heavy kettle and sauté the onions until golden. Add the garlic, juniper berries, coriander seed, and bay leaf, and sauté 5 minutes more.

2. Stir in the tomatoes, vinegar, water, chili pepper, salt, and chili powder, and simmer, covered, for 45 minutes. Stir and simmer, uncovered, for 10 minutes. Put mixture through a food mill or purée in a blender. Return to kettle, add grated chocolate, and simmer, uncovered, for 15 minutes, stirring.

3. Place pork, rib side down, in a roasting pan and ladle some of the sauce over it. Roast in a moderate oven, 350° F., for 3½ hours, basting with sauce and drippings. Spoon remaining barbecue sauce over each serving.

CHILI RIO GRANDE

(Makes 6–8 Servings)

>½ cup julienne strips of sow belly
>2 medium yellow onions, peeled and minced
>1 teaspoon ground cumin
>½ teaspoon orégano
>1 medium hot red pepper, crushed
>2 dashes Tabasco
>1 teaspoon paprika
>Dash cayenne pepper
>1 tablespoon chili powder
>1 teaspoon salt
>1 clove garlic, peeled and crushed
>1 (1 lb. 4 oz.) can red kidney beans
>2 cups canned tomatoes with basil
>1½ pounds ground beef chuck
>½ cup beef bouillon (optional)

1. Render the sow belly in a large, heavy skillet.

2. Add onions and sauté slowly until golden. Mix in cumin, orégano, hot red pepper, Tabasco, paprika, cayenne, chili powder, salt, and garlic.

3. Stir in kidney beans and tomatoes, and simmer slowly, stirring for ½ hour.

4. Mix in ground chuck and simmer ten minutes, stirring. Thin, if you like, with beef bouillon.

PUEBLO LAMB SHANKS

(Makes 6 Servings)

>3 lamb shanks, sawed in half
>Fresh ground pepper
>Flour for dusting
>¼ cup cooking oil
>5 dried juniper berries, crushed

2 yellow onions, peeled and chopped
2 cloves garlic, peeled and crushed
8 medium-sized mushrooms, wiped
1½ teaspoons salt
½ teaspoon basil
2 cups water or, if you like, 1 cup each water and
    dry white wine
1 (2 lb.) can tomatoes with basil

1. Season shanks with fresh ground pepper. Then dust with flour.

2. Heat the oil in a large, heavy kettle, add shanks and juniper berries. Slowly brown the meat on all sides, then transfer to paper toweling to drain.

3. Add onions and garlic to the kettle and sauté until golden.

4. Remove stems from mushrooms, chop, and add to the onions. Set mushroom caps aside.

5. Return shanks to the kettle; add salt, basil, water, and let boil slowly for 20 minutes, stirring occasionally.

6. Reduce heat, add mushroom caps and tomatoes, and simmer, uncovered, stirring occasionally, for 1½ hours.

Vegetables

Beans, like corn, were highly prized among tribes of the Southwest, who took great care to produce beans of as many colors as possible. The valued varieties were yellow, blue, red, white, multicolored, and black. The colors symbolized the six cardinal points—north, west, south, east, zenith and nadir, respectively. Beans were prepared in almost as many different ways as corn. They were soaked and served cold as salads, flattened and fried into cakes, or simmered long and slow with meats to make chilis and stews.

GREEN PEPPER AND PINK BEAN CASSEROLE

(Makes 4–6 Servings)

3 strips bacon, cut into julienne strips
1 green pepper, washed, cored and coarsely chopped
1 onion, peeled and chopped
1 clove garlic, peeled and crushed
1 tablespoon minced, cooked ham (optional)
1 cup canned tomatoes
1 teaspoon dark brown sugar
Pinch mace
Salt and coarsely ground black pepper to season
2 (1 lb.) cans of pink beans, drained

1. Brown the bacon slowly, add green pepper and onion, and sauté gently until tender.

2. Stir in garlic, minced ham (optional), tomatoes, brown sugar, mace, salt, and black pepper, and simmer, stirring, for about 10 minutes.

3. Mix tomato sauce with pink beans and transfer mixture to a 2-quart baking dish.

4. Bake, uncovered, for 45 minutes in a moderate oven, 350° F.

DILLED WAX BEANS

(Makes 4 Servings)

> *1 pound wax beans*
> *1 strip bacon*
> *1 teaspoon salt*
> *1 teaspoon honey*
> *1 tablespoon minced fresh dill*
> *6 tablespoons cider vinegar*

1. Wash the beans carefully, snap off ends, and remove strings. Place in a large saucepan with the bacon, cover with water, and simmer for about an hour or until tender.

2. Drain, remove bacon, and season with remaining ingredients. Serve hot as a vegetable or, if you like, chill and serve as a salad.

BEAN MOLD

(Makes 6 Servings)

> *½ pound dry pea beans*
> *2 strips bacon, diced and rendered (reserve drippings)*
> *½ cup corn meal*
> *1 teaspoon salt*
> *⅛ teaspoon fresh ground pepper*
> *½ teaspoon paprika*
> *4 dashes Tabasco*

1. Soak and cook the beans according to package directions, reserving 2 cups of their cooking water. If there are not 2 cups, add enough water to complete the measure.

2. Mash the beans and mix with the bacon, drippings, and corn meal.

3. Bring the 2 cups water to a boil, add the bean mixture along with the salt, pepper, paprika, and Tabasco. Reduce heat and simmer, stirring occasionally, for 25 minutes.

4. Pour into a 1½-quart casserole or baking dish, cool to room temperature, then chill until firm. Unmold and serve as a cold vegetable. This dish is a good potato substitute.

PUYÉ BEANS

(Makes 4 Servings)

> ½ cup cooking oil
> 1 green pepper, washed, cored and chopped
> 2 onions, peeled and chopped
> 2 cloves garlic, peeled and crushed
> 2 bay leaves
> 1 teaspoon salt
> ¼ teaspoon marjoram
> ¼ teaspoon coarsely ground black pepper
> 2 (1 lb.) cans black beans
> 1 cup rice, cooked according to package directions

1. Heat the oil in a large, heavy skillet and add the green pepper and about three fourths of the onions. Save remaining onions for garnish.

2. Add 1 clove garlic, the bay leaves, salt, marjoram, and black pepper, and sauté the mixture, stirring, until the onions and green pepper are tender.

3. Stir in the black beans, mashing them a little

with the back of a spoon, and simmer gently, stirring occasionally, for 30 minutes. Add second clove of garlic, and simmer about 10 minutes longer.

4. Remove bay leaves and serve black beans over rice. Top each serving with a sprinkling of the remaining chopped onions.

FRESH CORN PUFFS

(Makes about 4 Dozen)

4 ears fresh corn or 2 (10 oz.) packages frozen corn
  on the cob
3 cups shortening or oil for deep-fat frying
½ cup flour
1 teaspoon baking powder
½ teaspoon salt
¼ teaspoon paprika
⅛ teaspoon fresh ground pepper
3 eggs, beaten until light

1. Husk the corn, remove silks, and scrape kernels and pulp from the cob. If you use the frozen corn, thaw well before scraping. There should be about 1½ cups corn and pulp.

2. Place shortening or oil in a large kettle, and begin to heat slowly. For deep-fat frying the temperature should be 350° F. Use a deep-fat thermometer to determine exact temperature. It will take 10–15 minutes for the fat to become hot enough for frying.

3. Sift together the dry ingredients. Mix in the eggs and corn.

4. Drop batter from a teaspoon into the hot oil.

5. Fry the puffs until they are light and golden brown on all sides. Drain on paper toweling and serve.

BAKED VEGETABLES OF THE VINES

(Makes 4–6 Servings)

  2 onions, peeled and chopped
  2 cloves garlic, peeled and crushed
  ⅓ cup salad oil
  2 cucumbers, zucchini or yellow crookneck squash,
    washed and sliced
  1 large eggplant, washed and sliced
  2 green peppers, washed, cored and cut into strips
    about 1" wide
  2 tomatoes, washed, cored and sliced
  1 tablespoon salt
  ¼ teaspoon fresh ground black pepper
  1 teaspoon orégano
  ¼ teaspoon cumin seed
  ¼ teaspoon powdered dill
  3 tablespoons salad oil

1. In a flameproof oven casserole, sauté the onions and garlic in the ⅓ cup salad oil until golden. Remove half of the onions and set aside.

2. Mix together salt, fresh ground black pepper and herbs.

3. Lay sliced cucumbers on top of the onion mixture in the casserole; sprinkle with one third of the mixed seasonings and 1 tablespoon oil.

4. Add a layer of sliced eggplant; sprinkle with a third of the seasonings and 1 tablespoon oil.

5. Add a layer of green peppers; top with remaining seasonings and oil.

6. Cover casserole and bake for 1 hour in a moderate oven, 350° F.

7. Remove from oven, add a layer of sliced tomatoes, top with remaining onions, return to oven, and bake uncovered for 15 minutes more. Serve at once.

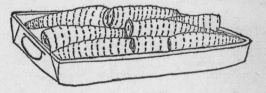

BAKED CARROTS

(Makes 4–6 Servings)

8 medium carrots
2 tablespoons butter or margarine
¼ teaspoon salt
⅛ teaspoon fresh ground pepper

1. Remove carrot tops. Wash carrots well but do not peel.

2. Parboil for 20 minutes or until a fork will just pierce them. Drain well.

3. Place carrots in an $8'' \times 8'' \times 2''$ baking dish, dot with butter, season with salt and pepper, and cover with aluminum foil. Bake in a moderate oven, 350° F., for 1 hour. Turn carrots once during baking and baste with the pan drippings.

Salads

KIDNEY BEAN SALAD

(Makes 6–8 Servings)

> 1 pound dried red kidney beans
> 3½ quarts water
> ¼ pound salt pork
> 1 yellow onion, peeled and sliced thin
> 2 cloves garlic, peeled and crushed
> ½ green pepper, washed and slivered
> ⅓ cup salad oil
> ¼ cup vinegar
> 1 teaspoon salt
> ¼ teaspoon black pepper

1. Soak the beans in 1½ quarts water for 3½ hours. Drain and rinse. Cover with the remaining water, add the salt pork, and simmer together for 2 hours. Drain and rinse well.

2. Place the beans in a large bowl. Add the onion, garlic, green pepper, salad oil, vinegar, salt, and black pepper, and toss well. Let marinate at room temperature for 1 hour. Toss again and serve.

MARINATED PEPPERS

(Makes 6 Servings)

DRESSING:

½ cup salad oil
⅓ cup tarragon vinegar
½ teaspoon crushed basil
½ teaspoon salt
Dash fresh ground black pepper
1 clove garlic, peeled and crushed
¼ teaspoon crushed dill seed
Pinch chervil
Pinch orégano

PEPPERS:

6 large sweet green peppers or 3 red and 3 green,
washed
Salt and fresh ground black pepper to season

1. Combine all dressing ingredients in a jar and shake to blend. Set aside and let stand at room temperature while you prepare the peppers.

2. Toast the peppers one at a time over an open flame (in the fireplace or over a gas burner). Spear the pepper with a long-handled fork and sear all over until skin is black. The peppers may also be toasted in the broiler. Place on broiler rack close to flame or unit and broil, turning frequently so that skins blacken evenly.

3. Place toasted peppers under cold running water and rub the blackened skin off.

4. Core peppers, drain well, cut into sixths, place in a large bowl, and sprinkle lightly with salt and fresh ground black pepper.

5. Pour about half of marinade over peppers (save remainder for a salad dressing later). Let peppers marinate at room temperature for about 20 minutes before serving.

MARINATED CUCUMBERS

(Makes 6 Servings)

> 2 cucumbers, washed and sliced paper thin
> 3 cups water
> 1 tablespoon salt

DRESSING:

> ¼ cup salad oil
> 2 tablespoons cider vinegar
> ⅛ teaspoon fresh ground pepper

1. Place the cucumbers, water, and salt in a large bowl, toss to mix, then soak for 1 hour. Drain cucumbers and pat dry between paper toweling.

2. Combine dressing ingredients, pour over cucumbers, and marinate in the refrigerator about 2 hours before serving. Toss and serve.

PEA BEAN SALAD

(Makes 4 Servings)

> ⅓ pound pea beans, washed, soaked, and cooked by
>   package directions
> 2 tablespoons salad oil
> 2 tablespoons cider vinegar
> ⅓ cup minced scallions or chives
> ½ green pepper, washed and minced

Drain the beans well and mix with remaining ingredients. Serve at room temperature, or chill and serve cold.

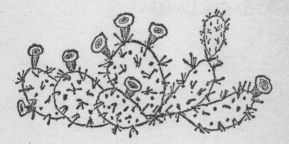

CACTUS SALAD

(Makes 4 Servings)

1 (7¼ oz.) can natural cactus in salt water, drained
1 (7 oz.) can pimiento, drained

DRESSING:

3 tablespoons salad oil
2 tablespoons tarragon vinegar
1 scallion, washed and minced
1 clove garlic, peeled and crushed
⅛ teaspoon fresh ground pepper

1. Arrange a bed of cactus on a small platter. Slice the pimiento into julienne strips and place over the cactus.

2. Mix together the dressing ingredients and pour over salad. Marinate in the refrigerator an hour before serving.

GIANT WHITE LIMA BEAN SALAD

(Makes 6 Servings)

> 1 pound dried giant white Lima beans, washed
> 2 quarts plus 1 cup water
> 1 tablespoon salt

DRESSING:

> ⅓ cup salad oil
> ¼ cup cider vinegar
> 3 cloves garlic, peeled and crushed
> 2 scallions, washed and sliced (include tops)
> ⅛ teaspoon fresh ground pepper

1. Place the beans in a large kettle, add 2 quarts water, and soak for 48 hours. Remove beans from soaking water, set the soaking water aside, and peel the beans.

2. Return the beans to the kettle along with their soaking water. Add 1 cup water and salt. Simmer slowly, covered, for 20 minutes. Drain.

3. Mix together all dressing ingredients and dress the beans. Toss; let marinate at room temperature for about 30 minutes before serving. Toss again and serve.

Breads and Spreads

Wheat came to the Southwest with the Spaniards and has been used by tribes there ever since for making the light, yeast-raised adobe breads, and the thin, flat tortillas. Adobe bread was and still is made in vast quantities, enough to last a tribe several weeks. One Indian recipe begins, "Take twenty-five pounds of flour . . ." At bread-baking time, fires are kindled in the beehive-shaped adobe ovens, or *hornos*, and the rounded loaves go into them on wooden slabs to bake long and slow until each loaf is puffed and light and golden brown. During ceremonies in the Pueblos, the women walk among the crowds passing out fresh loaves of bread before the feasting begins.

ADOBE BREAD

(Makes 2 Loaves)

> 1 (¼ oz.) package dry yeast
> ¼ cup warm water
> 2 tablespoons melted lard or shortening
> 1 teaspoon salt
> 4½ cups flour
> 1 cup water

1. Soften the yeast in the warm water in a large mixing bowl. Then mix in the melted lard or shortening and the salt.
2. Add flour alternately with the water, sifting the flour in a little at a time and beating well after

each addition to make a smooth mixture. You will probably have to knead in the final cup of flour.

3. Shape the dough into a ball, place in a greased bowl, brush lightly with melted lard or shortening, cover with a dry cloth, and set in a warm place to rise for about 1 hour.

4. When the dough has doubled in bulk, punch down, turn onto a floured board, and knead for about 5 minutes. Divide into two equal parts and shape into two round loaves on a well-oiled board or greased baking tin.

5. Cover the loaves with a dry cloth, set in a warm place, and let rise for 15 minutes.

6. Bake the bread in a hot oven, 400° F., for 50 minutes or until loaves are lightly browned and sound hollow when thumped. Cool; cut into wedges before serving.

TORTILLAS

(Makes about 12)

1½ cups masa harina*
2 teaspoons salt
2 teaspoons shortening
1¼ cups boiling water

YOU WILL ALSO NEED:

2 (6" square) pieces white muslin
2 heavy cutting boards

1. Mix together the dry ingredients. Melt the shortening in the boiling water, and mix into the masa. Beat well with a pastry blender for 10 minutes.

* This is a special, flourlike mixture for making tortillas. You can buy it in specialty food shops or in Spanish groceries.

2. Dampen the muslin. Lay ~~one~~ piece on a cutting board and smooth out.

3. Pinch off a piece of dough and roll into a ball about 1 inch in diameter. Place on the damp muslin, top with the second piece of muslin, then the second cutting board, and press flat. The tortillas should be almost paper-thin. Remove board, peel off muslin.

4. Place on a very hot rendered skillet or griddle, and brown, allowing about ½ minute per side. Repeat until all tortillas are made. Place in a napkin or linen towel to keep warm.

PIÑON CAKES

(Makes 6 Cakes)

> 2 cups piñon nuts
> ¾ cup water
> ½ teaspoon salt
> 2 tablespoons cooking oil

1. Purée the nuts in a blender, or chop and then roll with a rolling pin to a coarse meal.

2. Mix the piñon meal with the water and salt to form a stiff batter.

3. Let batter stand at room temperature for about an hour before cooking.

4. Place oil in a large heavy skillet; heat until a drop of water will sizzle. Drop piñon batter from a tablespoon, shaping into 6 cakes about 3½″ in diameter with a well-greased spatula.

5. Reduce heat and brown cakes slowly on each side. Serve hot or cold as a bread.

AVOCADO SPREAD

(Makes about 1½ Cups)

> 1 large ripe avocado
> 4 teaspoons cumin powder
> 1 tablespoon salad oil
> 1 teaspoon salt

Cut the avocado in half, remove seed, and scoop out the flesh. Mash well with a fork, then mix in remaining ingredients. Serve as a sauce for fish or as a spread for bread.

PEACH HONEY

(Makes about 1 Pint)

> 2 (12 oz.) packages frozen sliced peaches
> 2 cups sugar

1. Thaw the peaches well, purée, then place in a saucepan with the sugar.
2. Boil gently, stirring occasionally, for 2½ hours. Pour into 8-ounce jelly glasses. Peach honey is not a jelly but a thick syrup. Use it as you would honey—for cooking, for serving on bread, waffles, or pancakes.

APRICOT DRINK

(Makes 8–10 Servings)

>½ *pound dried apricots*
>2 *quarts water*
>1 *cup honey*

1. Simmer the apricots in 1½ quarts for 30 minutes.

2. Put through a food mill or purée in a blender until smooth.

3. Mix in the remaining water and honey, chill well, and serve iced.

JUNIPER TEA

(Makes 2 Quarts)

20 tender young sprigs of juniper, washed
2 quarts water

1. Place the juniper sprigs and water in a large saucepan, bring to a boil, cover, reduce heat, and let simmer gently for 15 minutes.
2. Turn heat off and let tea steep for 10 minutes.
3. Strain and serve.

THE FISHERMEN OF THE
PACIFIC NORTHWEST

THE FISHERMEN OF THE PACIFIC
NORTHWEST

Tribes of the Northwest Coast lived from the sea, and they lived richly. The Pacific served up whale, halibut, flounder, herring, sole, sturgeon and its dazzling red caviar, smelt, cod, olachen or candle fish, seal, and otter. It filled rocky coves and beaches with giant clams and crabs, succulent mussels and barnacles. The Pacific also drew the waterfowl, ducks and geese and gulls that followed sky trails along the coast and built nests among the outcropping cliffs. The sea was a garden, too, that produced year-round crops of kelp and seaweed. Finally, the sea water itself was a kind of *court bouillon*, fragrant, delicately salty, the perfect broth for soups and stews and vegetables.

The land was only slightly less abundant, for the Humboldt Current pushed warm, moist air over the area, making it luxuriant and green. In the mountains were deer, elk, bear, and wild goats; in the forests pheasant, plover, and lark; in the fields camass roots and wild carrots and potatoes. There were acorns and hazelnuts, wild salad greens both fragrant and pungent, and abundant supplies of sweet, juicy huckleberries, blackberries, raspberries, wild strawberries, blackcaps, salal, and salmonberries.

Most important of all foods to the Tlingit, Salish, Kwakiutl, Bella Coola, and other Northwest Coast tribes was fish, and most important of all fish was salmon. So much so that in some tongues the word for fish was the same as the word for salmon. Indians recognized "five tribes of salmon," and indeed, we know five species today. In summer, when the salmon run began, the rivers so swarmed with them that an old trader once observed, "They were so thick you could walk across on their backs."

Salmon were treated with great respect, for according to Indian belief, they were not fish at all but "spirit people" living in a magic village under the sea who were sent upriver each summer in fish disguise to feed the human race. The first salmon to be caught had to be carefully laid down on the river bank with its head upstream so that other fish would follow. In this way, it became the scout for its people and, as Indian legends tell, would beckon or warn the others to stay away according to the reception it had been given. Every Indian knew well this ceremony of the first salmon.

When the salmon were running, the women cleaned the fish with fresh ferns and cut them lengthwise with a knife of stone or mussel shell and skewered the steaks on sapling sticks to roast before an open fire.

Though it was the men who caught the salmon, it was traditionally the women who gathered shellfish and the eggs of seafowl along the coast. Oddly enough, the clams, mussels, and barnacles they gathered were never eaten raw but were steamed upon rocks that had been heated in cedar coals. Like salmon, they were also skewered and smoked for winter eating. This method of preserving food may account for the name Kwakiutl, which means "smoke of the world."

When it came to the fruits of the land, the lighter job of gathering again fell to the women. The berries they found there were easily eaten raw just as were the crisp greens. Vegetable roots, however, had to be boiled, and it is interesting that the Indians did not boil these vegetables directly over the fire but dropped hot stones in the water until it bubbled. Even more fascinating is the reason for this method. The pots were not of clay or stone or metal but were wooden buckets or baskets, which the women wove under water so tightly that they were absolutely leakproof. The Hupa and Tlingit still weave these exquisite baskets with characteristic geometric designs that have been traditional for centuries.

Though the sea was the great provider, whenever a family craved meat, the men would hunt for game. The women boiled fowl in baskets or spitted and roasted them over a fire. They surrounded giant roasts of deer, elk, and bear by three fires so that the meat browned evenly and slowly and became juicy and tender throughout. Sometimes young venison was fried, or small, tender cuts were wrapped with fat in a strip of cedar bark and set upon hot stones to steam.

With so much food abounding both on land and in the sea, it is not surprising that feasting was frequent and lavish among the tribes of the Northwest Coast. One of the most colossal of all feasts was the Potlatch, to which a chief would invite both his friends and his enemies to show how rich and powerful he and his tribe were. To do this, he would give away as many of the tribe's material possessions as he could, thereby cleverly placing each guest in his debt. To repay the debt, each guest was then obligated to stage a bigger and better Potlatch. And in the end, the tribe recouped its investment—with interest, usually two to one!

There were, of course, more usual family meals which were served twice a day and at which manners were extremely important. The upbringing of a girl was judged by watching her eat. If she took too much in her mouth at one time, exposed her teeth or raised her eyes from her food, she was considered ill-bred and a bad marriage prospect.

The leisurely life of the verdant Northwest Coast provided time for women to develop fish cookery to a fine art, for the men to carve gigantic cedar and hemlock monuments bearing totems or guardian spirits of the clans, sea mammals and monsters, birds and beasts that had made their life so abundant.

The foods served and the way of eating have not changed much today among these tribes. Those living on the Neah Bay and Yakima reservations of Washington, the Hupa of northern California or Saxman Indian Village of Alaska still live by the sea. Women here know as many ways to serve salmon as we do beef. And superb dishes they are—grilled salmon steaks, eggs scrambled with smoked salmon, smoked salmon soup, poached salmon in aspic, salmon cakes. Try them, you'll see.

Appetizers

Red caviar, one of the greatest delicacies among tribes of the Northwest Coast, was spread in the sun to dry until it became the consistency of a thick jam. It was then spread upon bread and relished for its salty flavor of the sea.

SMOKED SALMON OR RED CAVIAR SPREAD FOR BUCKSKIN BREAD

(Makes about 6 Servings)

> ¼ *pound sliced smoked salmon or 4 ounces red caviar*
> ½ *onion, peeled and minced*
> *Fresh ground pepper to season*
> *1 recipe Buckskin Bread**

70

1. Lay slices of smoked salmon on the buckskin bread, or spread with red caviar.

2. Top with a sprinkling of minced onion, and season with fresh ground pepper.

3. Cut into thin wedges, and serve as an hors d'oeuvre.

OCTOPUS FRITTERS

(Makes 8 Servings)

> 2 small octopuses weighing about 1½ pounds each, cleaned
> 2 yellow onions, peeled and minced
> 1 teaspoon salt
> 2 eggs
> 1 cup flour
> ⅓ cup cooking oil

1. Drop the octopuses into a large kettle of rapidly boiling water and boil, uncovered, for 20 minutes. Drain and plunge into ice water. Using a coarse brush, scrape away the purple skin. Cut off the legs and chop fine. Discard the heads.

2. Mix together the onions, salt, eggs, and flour to form a batter. Then stir in the minced octopus. Shape into flat cakes about 3″ in diameter.

3. Heat the oil in a large, heavy skillet, and brown the octopus fritters well on each side. Serve hot with butter.

SMOKED SALMON SOUP

(Makes 4 Servings)

> 1 pound sliced smoked salmon
> 1 quart water
> ⅛ teaspoon fresh ground pepper
> ¾ cup young spinach leaves, washed

1. Break the salmon into bite-sized pieces, and place in a large saucepan with the water and pepper. Simmer gently, stirring occasionally, for 15 minutes.

2. Add the spinach and simmer for 5 minutes longer.

SCALLION SOUP

(Makes 6 Servings)

8 scallions, washed and sliced (include tops)
8 dried juniper berries
2 (5.4 gram) packages instant chicken broth
½ teaspoon salt
6 cups water

Place all ingredients in a large saucepan, bring to a boil, then reduce heat and simmer for 30 to 40 minutes. Serve hot.

FISH AND SPINACH BROTH

(Makes 8–10 Servings)

1 large potato, peeled and quartered
1 large onion, peeled and quartered
2 quarts water
6 peppercorns
10 dried juniper berries
1 pound fresh spinach, washed and picked over to remove coarse stems
4 fillets flounder, sole or other delicate white fish or 2 (12 oz.) packages frozen flounder fillets
10 fresh mint leaves, washed
2 teaspoons salt

1. Place the potato, onion, water, peppercorns, and juniper berries in a large, heavy kettle, and bring to a boil. Reduce heat and simmer for about 50 minutes or until the potato is tender. Break up the potato into bite-sized pieces, and mash the juniper berries with a spoon against the sides of the kettle.

2. Add the fresh fish or frozen fillets and simmer for 8 minutes, breaking up the fish into small pieces.

3. Stir in the spinach, mint, and salt, and simmer for 5 minutes more. Serve steaming hot.

Main Dishes

SALMON CAKES

(Makes 6–8 Servings)

1 (1 lb.) can salmon, flaked (include liquid)
4 juniper berries, crushed
⅓ cup corn meal
2 eggs, lightly beaten
⅔ cup milk

Mix all ingredients together, spoon into a well-greased muffin tin, and bake in a moderate oven, 350° F., for 30 minutes. Serve hot or cold.

SALMON CHOWDER

(Makes 6–8 Servings)

4 potatoes, peeled and diced
6 cups water
1¼ pounds fresh salmon, cut into chunks
2 teaspoons salt
⅛ teaspoon fresh ground pepper

1. Simmer the potatoes in the water for 40 minutes or until tender.

2. Add remaining ingredients, and simmer for 10 minutes more.

HALIBUT ASPIC

(Makes about 5 Cups)

> 6 heads of halibut or trout
> 6 cups water
> 2 teaspoons salt
> ⅓ cup chopped water cress
> 1 tablespoon minced fresh dill
> ⅛ teaspoon fresh ground pepper

1. Boil the fish heads with the water and salt for 1 hour. Strain and stir in the water cress, dill, and pepper.

2. Pour into a mold and chill until firm or use for glazing poached salmon.

POACHED SALMON IN HALIBUT ASPIC

(Makes 4–6 Servings)

> 1 recipe Halibut Aspic *
> 4 slices fresh salmon cut 1¼" thick

1. Poach the salmon gently in the halibut aspic for 10 minutes.

2. Place in a large, shallow, rectangular baking dish, and cover with the aspic. Chill until firm and serve.

FLOUNDER WITH MUSSEL SAUCE

(Makes 8 Servings)

2 dozen mussels in the shell, scrubbed
½ cup water
3 eggs, beaten lightly
1 cup corn meal
2 teaspoons salt
⅛ teaspoon fresh ground pepper
8 fillets of flounder, sole, or other delicate white fish
½ cup plus 2 tablespoons butter or margarine
½ cup minced fresh chives

1. Place the mussels on a rack in a large, heavy kettle. Add the water, bring to a boil, cover, reduce heat, and steam the mussels for 15 minutes. Remove mussels from the shell, and chop fine. Reserve ¼ cup of the cooking water.

2. Place the lightly beaten eggs in a pie plate. Mix the corn meal with the salt and fresh ground pepper, and place in a second pie plate.

3. Dip the fillets first in the egg and then in the corn-meal mixture so that they are lightly but evenly coated. Then brown the fillets on both sides in the ½ cup butter or margarine in a large, heavy skillet.

4. In a small skillet, melt the 2 tablespoons butter or margarine; add the minced chives and mussels and the ¼ cup mussel-cooking water. Simmer together for about 5 minutes.

5. Serve the browned fillets on a large platter, topped with the mussel sauce.

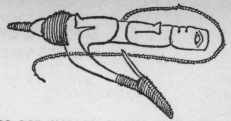

EGGS SCRAMBLED WITH SMOKED SALMON

(Makes 4 Servings)

>   6 eggs
>   ⅛ teaspoon pepper
>   1 tablespoon minced chives
>   2 tablespoons butter or margarine
>   ½ pound sliced smoked salmon, cut into julienne
>   strips

1. Beat the eggs with the pepper until foamy. Stir in the minced chives.

2. Melt the butter or margarine in a large skillet, pour in the egg mixture, add the smoked salmon, and cook slowly, stirring, until the eggs are soft-cooked.

BROILED ALASKAN KING CRAB

(Makes 2–4 Servings)

>   1 pound frozen Alaskan king crab meat, thawed
>   3 tablespoons melted butter
>   1 tablespoon minced chives
>   Salt and pepper to season

Drain the crab well, place on a broiler pan, and top with butter and half of the chives. Broil for 4 minutes, turn, add remaining chives, baste with drippings, and broil for 4 minutes longer. Salt and pepper to season.

STEAMED MUSSELS WITH BUTTER SAUCE

(Makes 4–6 Servings)

>   2½ dozen large mussels in the shell
>   2 cups water
>   ½ cup butter or margarine
>   3 tablespoons minced chives

1. Scrub the mussels thoroughly with a stiff brush in cold water. Then place on a rack in the bottom of a large kettle and add the water. When the water comes to a boil, cover the kettle and steam the mussels for 15 minutes.

2. Meanwhile, place the butter and chives in a small saucepan, and heat slowly until the butter is melted.

3. Arrange the mussels on a large platter centered with a bowl of the chive butter. It is used as a dip.

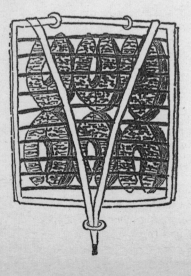

GRILLED SALMON STEAKS

(Makes 6 Servings)

> 6 salmon steaks 1 inch thick, cut crosswise
> 30 dried juniper berries
> Salt and fresh ground pepper to season
> Lemon wedges (optional)

1. Into each steak, press 5 juniper berries, distributing them so that their aroma will permeate the fish. Press the berries about halfway down into the flesh.

2. Grill the salmon over glowing coals (about 5 to 6 inches from the heat) for 3 minutes on each side. To broil in the oven, allow about 4 to 5 minutes for each side.

3. Season each steak with salt and fresh ground pepper.

4. Serve, if you like, with lemon wedges.

POACHED SALMON

(Makes 6 Servings)

> 6 (1″) cross-cut salmon steaks
> 6 medium mushrooms, wiped and sliced
> 2 teaspoons minced fresh parsley
> 2 scallions, finely chopped (include tops)
> 1 sweet red pepper, washed, cored and finely chopped
> 1 quart canned chicken broth
> 2 teaspoons salt
> ¼ teaspoon fresh ground black pepper
> Lemon wedges (optional)

1. Simmer the mushrooms, parsley, scallions, and

red pepper in the chicken broth for 10 minutes. Season with salt and fresh ground black pepper. Cool broth to room temperature or, if you wish, prepare broth a day or two ahead and refrigerate until you are ready to poach the salmon.

2. Place salmon steaks in a large skillet, cover with broth, and simmer (do not boil) for 15 to 20 minutes.

3. Serve each salmon steak topped with a little broth. Garnish, if you like, with lemon. The poached salmon is delicious served hot or cold.

ROAST PHEASANT STUFFED WITH GRAPES AND NUTS

(Makes 4 Servings)

2 (3 lb.) pheasants, dressed and larded
¾ cup butter or margarine
½ teaspoon thyme
1 tablespoon salt
18 dried juniper berries, crushed
⅛ teaspoon fresh ground pepper
2 pounds seedless grapes, washed
1 cup mixed broken nut meats (walnuts, hazelnuts, hickory, or piñon)

1. Remove any pinfeathers from the birds and singe off hairs.

2. Melt the butter or margarine and mix in thyme, salt, crushed juniper berries, and pepper. Rub the birds well inside and out with the seasoned butter.

3. Mash half of the grapes, then mix with remaining grapes, the nuts, and remaining seasoned butter. Stuff each bird very full, skewer openings shut, and truss. Wrap remaining stuffing in aluminum foil.

4. Place birds on a rack in an open roasting pan and roast in a very hot oven, 425° F., for 15 minutes. The foil-wrapped stuffing can be placed in the roasting pan beside the birds. Baste with drippings, reduce heat to moderate, 350° F., and continue to roast for 30 minutes more or until birds are tender. Baste every 10 minutes with drippings.

Vegetables

When traders moved west across the United States and introduced *beets, turnips,* and *potatoes* to the northwest country, the Indian women there prepared them as they did camass and other roots that is, by baking or roasting them whole in the skin. Doing so produced a sweeter flavor and a more succulent texture.

BAKED BEETS

(Makes 4–6 Servings)

8 medium to large beets
¼ cup butter or margarine
¼ cup honey
½ teaspoon salt

1. Scrub the beets well with a stiff brush, but do not peel. Remove tops (save for a salad or use as a cooked green vegetable).

2. Parboil the beets for about 45 minutes or until a fork will just pierce them. Drain well.

3. Place beets in a baking dish, dot with butter, and pour honey over all. Season with salt. Cover and bake in a moderate oven, 350° F., for 1 hour and 25 minutes, basting occasionally.

BAKED TURNIPS

(Makes 6–8 Servings)

1½ pounds small white turnips
¼ cup butter or margarine
½ teaspoon salt
¼ teaspoon coarse ground pepper

1. Wash turnips well and trim off stems. Parboil for 20 to 30 minutes or until a fork will just pierce them.

2. Place in a shallow baking dish, dot with butter or margarine, and sprinkle with salt and pepper.

3. Cover and bake in a hot oven, 400° F., for 30 minutes.

POTATOES BAKED IN HOT ASHES

(Makes 6 Servings)

6 Idaho potatoes

1. Wash the potatoes well and wrap in heavy aluminum foil.

2. Place in glowing coals. Charcoal briquettes prepared for broiling meat work well.

3. Bake for 1 hour, turning 3 times while the potatoes bake.

4. Serve hot with lots of butter, salt, and pepper.

Salads

In fields along the Northwest Coast grew an assortment of fragrant *wild greens* much like spinach in color, texture, and flavor. Women gathered them to use in making soups, salads, and vegetable dishes. A favorite way of preparing them was to wilt them with hot fat or fish oil.

WILTED SPINACH SALAD

(Makes 6 Servings)

DRESSING:

2 slices bacon, cut into julienne strips
⅓ cup red wine vinegar
1 scallion, washed and sliced thin
½ teaspoon orégano
Pinch fresh ground pepper
1 teaspoon salt
2 cloves garlic, peeled and crushed
Juice of ½ lemon
⅓ cup bottled chili sauce

SALAD:

1 (10 oz.) package washed and prepared fresh spinach
1 scallion, washed and sliced thin (include some tops)

1. Brown the bacon slowly in a large skillet.

2. While the bacon browns, pick over the spinach, removing any coarse stems. Place spinach and sliced scallion in a large salad bowl.

3. To the bacon, add remaining dressing ingredients, and heat, stirring, just until steaming.

4. Pour quickly over the spinach, toss well, and serve at once.

MINT SALAD

(Makes 6–8 Servings)

SALAD:

2 cups washed, chopped water cress
2 cups washed, chopped romaine
1 cup washed, diced radishes
4 scallions, washed and sliced thin (include tops)

DRESSING:

½ cup salad oil
¼ cup tarragon vinegar
½ cup finely chopped fresh mint
1 teaspoon salt
¼ teaspoon fresh ground pepper

1. Place salad ingredients in a large bowl.

2. Mix together all dressing ingredients (the dressing will be better if made an hour or two before serving time).

3. Pour dressing over salad, toss, and let stand for 10 minutes. Toss again and serve.

Breads

BUCKSKIN BREAD

(Makes 6 Servings)

>   2 cups flour
>   1 teaspoon baking powder
>   1 teaspoon salt
>   1 cup water

1. Sift together the dry ingredients, then quickly mix in the water.

2. Press the dough into a 9″ pie pan and bake in a hot oven, 400° F., for 25 minutes. Cut into wedges and serve. This is the perfect bread for "sopping up" potlikker and gravies.

Desserts

It may seem odd to associate *fritters* and *dumplings* with Indian cookery. Yet Indian women have been mixing berries and batters, wrapping bits of fruit in dough and deep-fat frying them for as long as they have had fruit, flour, and fat for deep frying.

BLUEBERRY FRITTERS

(Makes about 4 Dozen)

>   2 (9 oz.) packages frozen blueberries
>   4 cups flour
>   ¾ cup sugar
>   3½ teaspoons baking powder
>   3 cups shortening or oil for deep-fat frying
>   5 eggs

1. Thaw the blueberries well; drain off syrup and save.

2. Sift together the dry ingredients. Measure the blueberry syrup. There should be about ½ cup. If not, add water to complete the measure.

3. Place shortening or oil in a heavy, deep kettle and begin heating gradually. By the time you have finished mixing the fritters, the fat will register 350° F. on a deep-fat-frying thermometer and be just right for frying.

4. Beat the eggs with the blueberry syrup until foamy. Mix quickly into the dry ingredients, and fold in the berries.

5. Drop from a tablespoon into the hot fat. Turn the fritters frequently as they cook so that they become chocolate brown on all sides. Drain on paper toweling and serve hot.

CRANBERRY FRITTERS

(Makes about 9 Dozen)

1 cup fresh cranberries, washed and drained well
3 cups flour
1¼ cups sugar
2 tablespoons baking powder
½ teaspoon salt
1 cup plus 2 tablespoons milk
3 cups shortening or oil for deep-fat frying

1. Place the cranberries on paper toweling and dry well.

2. Sift together the dry ingredients and mix in the milk, a little at a time, to make a stiff dough.

3. Flour your hands well, pinch off a small piece of dough (about 1 teaspoon), place a cranberry in the center, and roll into a ball with the cranberry inside. The balls should be about the size of large marbles.

4. Place the shortening or oil in a deep, heavy kettle, and heat till it registers 375° F. on a deep-fat-frying thermometer.

5. Drop the fritters into the hot fat and fry, turning, until deep golden brown on all sides. Drain on paper toweling. This really works best as a two-woman operation, with one shaping the fritters and the other frying them.

The two favorite ways of preparing the *wild berries* that grew in profusion along the Northwest Coast were to pound or mash them into a purée or poach them in a syrup. Both dishes were served hot or cold.

STRAWBERRIES POACHED IN HONEY SYRUP

(Makes 4–6 Servings)

> *1 quart fresh strawberries, washed and stemmed*
> *¼ cup honey*
> *2 tablespoons sugar*
> *⅔ cup water*

1. Pick over the berries carefully, rejecting any that are blemished or overripe.
2. Place the honey, sugar, and water in a saucepan, and boil rapidly for 5 minutes. Reduce heat, drop in the whole berries, and simmer for 5 minutes.
3. Turn off the heat and let the berries cool to room temperature in the syrup. Serve warm or cold, ladling syrup over each portion.

WHIPPED RASPBERRIES AND HONEY

(Makes 4–6 Servings)

> *1 quart fresh raspberries, washed*
> *½ cup honey*

1. Mash the berries in the honey, or purée in a blender until smooth.
2. Chill well and serve. Make the portions small; the dessert is rich. This, actually, is a dessert soup.

THE WANDERING HUNTERS
OF THE PLAINS

THE WANDERING HUNTERS OF
THE PLAINS

West of the Mississippi, farmland gives way to the prairie where, less than a hundred years ago, the Plains Indians followed the great buffalo, turning it into food, clothing, and shelter. This was the land of the Siouan tribes whose feathered war bonnets and beaded buckskin clothes have become for us the very symbol of the American Indian today.

These were migratory tribes, particularly the Dakota and Cheyenne, who tracked the buffalo carrying their homes and possessions with them on dog-pulled travois. The great westward sweep of Plains was rugged country, for the most part dry and difficult to cultivate. However, in the Mississippi and Missouri river valleys, where the land was fertile enough to farm, the Osage, Mandan, Kiowa, and others led more settled lives centered around their crops of corn, beans, tomatoes, and squash.

George Catlin, journeying up the Missouri River in 1832, wrote one of the first colorful descriptions of the Plains and its people: "The buffalo herds, which graze in almost countless numbers on these beautiful prairies, afford an abundance of meat; and so much is it preferred to all other, that the deer, the elk, and the antelope sport upon the prairies in herds in the greatest security; as the Indians seldom kill them unless they want their skins for a dress. The buffalo is a noble animal, that roams over the vast prairies, from the Borders of Mexico on the south, to Hudson's Bay on the north. Their size is somewhat above that of our common bullock, and their flesh of a delicious flavour, resembling and equalling that of fat beef . . ."

To the Siouan and Blackfoot tribes who dominated the Plains, buffalo was as much the staff of life as corn was to the Southwest. Each spring, when migrations brought the buffalo back to their lands, they welcomed it eagerly, for it meant fresh meat once again. Women roasted giant haunches over their campfires; they broiled steaks, made stews of the shanks and brisket. The ribs and joints, rich with marrow, were simmered into savory soups. No part of the animal was ever wasted.

When buffalo was not available, the men hunted venison and rabbit, which their women roasted over glowing coals or made into thick stews with wild rice or dumplings. Sometimes there was fresh brook trout, which the women would skewer and broil or fry in hot fat. When there was no meat, the women hunted fowl eggs, an excellent source of protein, which they would boil for eating out of the hand or scramble with wild onions. For vegetables they either stone-boiled or baked roots in hot ashes. Many wild greens were simply eaten raw or simmered in stock until tender. Though uncomplicated, you can see that the recipes of the Plains tribes were hearty.

After taking part in a Mandan feast, Catlin wrote: "The simple feast which was spread before us consisted of three dishes only, two of which were served in wooden bowls, and the third in an earthen vessel . . . The last contained a quantity of *pem-i-can* and *marrow-fat;* and one of the former held a fine brace of buffalo ribs, delightfully roasted; and the other was filled with a kind of paste or pudding, made of the flour of the *'pomme blanch,'* as the French call it, a delicious turnip of the prairie, finely flavoured with the buffalo berries which are collected in great quantities in this country, and used with divers dishes in cooking, as we in civilized countries use dried currants, which they very much resemble."

Buffalo berries were a favorite among the Plains tribes. The bushes ran rampant over the prairie, their branches bent to the ground under the weight of scarlet clusters of berries. The harvest season was late fall, after the first frost had mellowed the flavor of the tart berries and made them sweeter. The most popular methods of preparing these berries, which are very much like cranberries, were to dry and mix them with jerky into pemmican and to mash them into a sauce which was ladled over buffalo meat—hence their name, buffalo berries.

Among the farming Plains Indians, from the Osage and Witchita to the Mandan, there was corn —to be roasted long and slow in the husk until each kernel was sweet and milky; parched until crunchy, golden, and nutlike; or pounded into a meal for making bread and thickening stews. One variety of corn had ears no longer than a man's thumb, so tender and sweet they could be eaten like grapes.

The Mandan, Osage, and other farming tribes lived in grass or earth lodges, shaped very much like Eskimo igloos. The tipis, on the other hand, belonged to the Sioux and other tribes who followed the buffalo, and some of their encampments included as many as six hundred of these brilliantly decorated, conical tents.

The tipi was as much temple as home, its floor representing the earth from which the Indians lived, its walls the sky, and its poles the sacred paths between earth and the spirit world. The Sioux tribes observed a strict tipi etiquette: if the flap was open, friends were welcome to enter; if not, they were to announce their presence by rattling the covering and wait for an invitation. Two crossed sticks hung above the door indicated that the occupants were either not at home or not receiving company.

Though each tipi had its own center fire, the Sioux preferred to cook out of doors and did so whenever the weather was good. Women dug large holes in the ground, lined them with stones, and covered them with fires until the stones were steaming hot. They then spread a fresh hide over the stones and laid chunks of meat on the skin. When the skin had been folded over, sealing in the meat, the women filled the pit with earth and left it undisturbed for hours until the meat was done. Sometimes sweet leaves of sassafras or maple were used to line the pits instead of skins, particularly in later years when there were hams to bake.

Feasting was popular among Plains tribes, and here, too, a strict code of etiquette was practiced. At the feast of the first buffalo, for example, each invited guest brought his own dishes and utensils, then took them home afterward and washed then. The women sat along the south of the tipi, the men on the north; and the host waited upon them, serving the men first. He was not free to sit down and enjoy his own meal until after the needs of each guest had been answered.

Without the buffalo, the Plains tribes would have been extremely poor because their land was the most difficult to cultivate. The Plains women did not have the gardens and orchards that the Pueblo women had, they had none of the elegant seafood of the East, the succulent fruits of the South, nor the salmon of the Northwest. Still they developed recipes that have become very much a part of the American menu today. The elegant, long-grained wild rice was theirs, and they used it as we do today for stuffing game birds or as an accompaniment for venison. They were artists at both game and campfire cooking as you will discover in the following recipes. Plains dishes are for the most part simple, but then the most eloquent foods are often the simplest.

Soups

One of the most special and popular corn dishes is *dried corn soup,* made by soaking dried kernels in water, then boiling them in broth to make a nourishing, nutlike soup. In some tribes, dried corn soup was served at the height of the Green Corn Ceremony.

DRIED CORN SOUP

(Makes 6 Servings)

> 1 ear dried blue and white or other corn, removed
>   from the cob
> 7 cups water
> 1 (2" ✕ 1") strip fat back, sliced
> ½ (5 oz.) jar dried beef
> ⅛ teaspoon fresh ground pepper

1. Soak the corn in 2 cups water for 48 hours.

2. Place the corn and its soaking water in a large saucepan. Add the remaining water and the fat back, and simmer, covered, for about 3 hours and 50 minutes or until the corn is tender but not soft.

3. Mix in the dried beef and pepper, and simmer, stirring, for 10 minutes more. Serve hot.

TROUT CONSOMMÉ

(Makes 4–6 Servings)

> 8 leftover cooked trout heads
> 5 cups water
> 1 teaspoon salt
> ⅛ teaspoon fresh ground pepper

1. Place all ingredients in a saucepan, and simmer slowly for ½ hour.

2. Strain and serve hot, or chill and serve cold as an aspic.

WATER CRESS SOUP

(Makes 4–6 Servings)

> 2 (12 oz.) cans chicken consommé
> 1 cup water
> 5 scallions, washed and sliced thin (include some
>   tops)
> 2 cups water cress leaves and tender shoots, washed
> Fresh ground pepper to season
> Sliced lemon or lime (optional)

1. Place chicken consommé and water in a saucepan; bring to a boil.

2. Add scallions, reduce heat to low, and simmer 3–4 minutes.

3. Add water cress leaves, turn heat off, and let soup steep about 1 minute.

4. Serve at once, seasoning each helping with fresh ground pepper and garnishing, if you like, with slices of lemon or lime. Or chill soup, skim off fat, and serve cold.

CORN CHOWDER

(Makes 4–6 Servings)

> ½ pound salt pork cut into julienne strips
> 1 onion, peeled and chopped
> ½ green pepper, washed, cored and chopped

1 potato, peeled and diced
2 tablespoons butter or margarine
½ teaspoon salt
⅛ teaspoon fresh ground black pepper
2 (10 oz.) packages frozen kernel corn
3 tablespoons minced parsley
2½ cups milk or light cream

1. Render the salt pork slowly in a large, heavy skillet.

2. Add the onion, green pepper, potato, and butter or margarine, and sauté slowly for 15–20 minutes or until potato is tender.

3. Add salt, black pepper, and corn, and heat, stirring, until corn has thawed.

4. Stir in parsley and milk or light cream, and simmer gently, stirring, until corn is done. Do not boil. Serve at once.

CORN AND DRIED BEEF SOUP

(Makes 6–8 Servings)

6 ears sweet corn
1 quart water
1 (5 oz.) jar dried beef
½ cup julienne strips of green pepper
2 scallions, washed and sliced thin (include tops)
⅛ teaspoon fresh ground black pepper
2 teaspoons sugar

1. Husk the corn and cut the kernels from the cob. Then scrape the pulp and milk from the cob.

2. Place the corn, milk, and pulp in a large, shallow kettle. Add water and simmer gently for 40 minutes. You can, if you like, substitute 2 (10 oz.) packages frozen whole kernel corn for the fresh and simmer for 10 minutes or until the corn is just tender.

3. Add beef and green pepper and simmer 20 minutes.

4. Mix in scallions, black pepper, and sugar, and simmer for 5 minutes longer.

Turtles and *turtle eggs* were relished by tribes of the Plains. Among the species available were snappers, and painted and wood turtles, and along the Gulf, the giant sea turtles. The meat was considered a "good medicine" and was simmered into soups or stews. Turtle broth was thought to be a remedy for throat troubles and excellent food for newborn babies. Warriors made a point of eating turtle before going into battle, for they believed that it protected them and made them difficult to kill.

TURTLE SOUP

(Makes 4 Servings)

1 pound frozen turtle or terrapin meat
2 scallions, washed and sliced (include tops)
2½ quarts water
1 (4.5 gram) package instant beef broth
½ teaspoon salt

1. Place the turtle or terrapin meat in a large, heavy kettle. Add the scallions and 1½ quarts water. Simmer together gently for 2 hours.

2. Remove the meat from the broth, and dice. Return to the broth. Add 1 quart water, the instant beef broth, and the salt, and simmer for 2 hours longer or until the meat is tender. Serve hot.

A seasonal delicacy among the Plains Indians was *mushrooms*, which the women fried, baked, or simmered into broth. One early soup recipe was simple but classic: "Boil the mushrooms, drain, add more hot water and also some kind of meat. Boil until the meat is cooked." Sometimes, when meat was not available, women made the soup by boiling fresh mushrooms with wild onions in meat stock.

MUSHROOM SOUP

(Makes 6 Servings)

> ½ pound mushrooms, wiped and coarsely chopped
> 1 sprig mint, washed
> 2 scallions, washed and sliced (include tops)
> 6 cups water
> 3 (4.5 gram) packages instant beef broth
> 1 tablespoon butter
> 1 teaspoon salt

Place all ingredients in a large saucepan, bring to a boil, then reduce heat and simmer for 30 to 40 minutes. Serve hot.

BROILED RAINBOW TROUT

(Makes 6 Servings)

> 6 (½ lb.) rainbow trout, cleaned
> 3 tablespoons butter
> ½ teaspoon salt
> ⅛ teaspoon fresh ground pepper
> ¼ cup minced parsley

Rub each fish well with butter. Broil for 4 to 5 minutes on a side. Baste with the drippings, season with salt and pepper, and top with minced parsley.

FRIED RAINBOW TROUT

(Makes 6 Servings)

> 6 (½ lb.) rainbow trout, cleaned
> 3 eggs, lightly beaten
> 2 cups corn meal
> 1 teaspoon salt
> ⅛ teaspoon fresh ground pepper
> ⅓ cup cooking oil

1. Dip the trout into the beaten eggs, then in the corn meal, which has been mixed with the salt and pepper. Be sure that each fish is lightly coated with the seasonal meal.

2. Heat the oil in a large heavy skillet until a drop of water will sizzle. Fry the fish for 4 to 5 minutes on a side.

LAMB STEW WITH
SQUAW BREAD DUMPLINGS

(Makes 4–6 Servings)

>4 pounds lamb shoulder (or beef chuck) cut into
>   1½" cubes
>⅓ cup vegetable oil
>1 onion, peeled and chopped
>2 cloves garlic, peeled and crushed
>6 dried juniper berries, crushed
>5 cups water
>1 teaspoon salt
>¼ teaspoon fresh ground pepper
>Squaw Bread dough* (use ½ recipe)

1. Heat the oil in a large, heavy kettle (one with a tight-fitting lid). Add lamb, and brown on all sides.

2. Add onion, garlic, and juniper berries, and sauté until the onion is golden.

3. Pour in 2½ cups water, season with salt and pepper, cover, and simmer for 2 hours, stirring occasionally.

4. When the lamb is tender, shape the Squaw Bread dough into balls about the size of walnuts.

5. Add 2½ cups water to the stew, bring to a rapid boil, drop in the dumplings, cover the kettle tightly, and boil for 12 minutes without uncovering. Serve at once.

Game did much to fill the larders of the Plains tribes. There was deer, buffalo, bear, squirrel, rabbit, beaver, and muskrat. Indians were particular about the game they ate and usually took only those animals which fed upon grass. There were two principal ways of preparing game: boiling it into stew or broiling it on pointed sticks. For larger game, the Sioux and others wove a grill of green saplings and hung it above the fire. The fat of the animals was saved for cooking, and that used for frying bear, raccoon, and porcupine was collected and kept for relieving chest cramps and anointing infants.

CHARCOAL-BROILED BUFFALO STEAKS

(Makes 6 Servings)

6 buffalo steaks each about 1" thick (if you use the frozen buffalo steaks, thaw thoroughly before using)
Salt
Pepper

1. Place the steaks in a long-handled broiling rack, and broil about 3" from glowing coals for 2 minutes on a side.
2. Sprinkle with salt and fresh ground pepper to season.

BROILED VENISON STEAK

(Makes 4–6 Servings)

4 vension steaks cut 1" thick

1. Place the steaks in a long-handled broiling rack and broil about 3" from glowing coals for 2 to

3 minutes on a side, depending upon how rare you like your meat.

2. Serve with salt and fresh ground pepper to season.

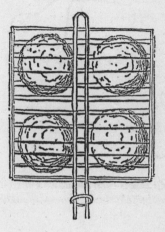

BROILED REINDEERBURGERS

(Makes 4 Servings)

1½ pounds ground venison
16 strips fat back or bacon about 2" long
3 scallions, minced
4 round buns, toasted
¼ cup dry red wine
Salt to taste
Fresh ground pepper to taste

1. Shape the ground venison into four thick patties.

2. Lay two strips fat back or bacon on the top of

each patty, then arrange patties bacon side down on a long-handled rack. Place two strips fat back or bacon on face up side of the patties. Secure in rack, and broil for two minutes on a side over glowing coals. Broil about 4″ away from the coals.

3. Remove at once to toasted buns. Top each with scallions, 1 tablespoon dry red wine, and a generous sprinkling of salt and pepper.

NOTE: Reindeerburgers may be pan-broiled in bacon drippings—about 2–3 minutes per side for rare; or they may be broiled in the oven. For oven broiling, top each patty with strips of fat back or bacon, and allow about 3–4 minutes per side for rare.

ROAST SADDLE OF VENISON

(Makes 6–8 Servings)

1 (3¾ lb.) saddle of venison (have the butcher saw through the backbone so that each serving may be carved without difficulty)
Peppercorns
Dried juniper berries
4 strips of lard or bacon cut ⅛″ thick

1. Stud the venison well with peppercorns and juniper berries.

2. Lay strips of lard or bacon over the meat, and secure with toothpicks.

3. Stand the saddle on a rack in a roasting pan.

4. Roast, basting frequently, for 40 minutes in a very hot oven, 450°F.

5. Carve so that each serving is one rib thick. Serve with some of the drippings. Wild rice is the perfect accompaniment.

GREEN PEPPERS STUFFED WITH VENISON

(Makes 6 Servings)

6 green peppers
2½ cups diced leftover cooked venison
6 mushrooms, wiped and coarsely chopped
2 scallions, washed and sliced thin
5 tablespoons bacon drippings or melted butter or
    margarine
1 teaspoon salt
⅛ teaspoon black pepper

1. Wash the green peppers, core, and chop the cores. Mix the chopped cores with the venison, chopped mushrooms, sliced scallions, bacon drippings, salt, and black pepper.

2. Stuff the peppers with the venison mixture, stand in a shallow baking pan, and bake in a moderate oven, 350°F., for 45 minutes.

VENISON AND WILD RICE STEW

(Makes 6–8 Servings)

> 3½ pounds shoulder of venison, cut into 2" cubes
> 2 quarts water
> 2 yellow onions, peeled and quartered
> 2 teaspoons salt
> ⅛ teaspoon fresh ground pepper
> 1½ cups wild rice, washed in cold water

1. Place the venison, water, and onions in a large, heavy kettle, and simmer, uncovered, for 3 hours or until venison is tender.
2. Mix in the salt, pepper, and wild rice, cover, and simmer for 20 minutes.
3. Stir the mixture, then simmer, uncovered for about 20 minutes more or until rice is tender and most of the liquid absorbed.

SAUTÉED BRAINS

(Makes 4 Servings)

> 2 eggs
> 2 tablespoons corn meal
> 1 teaspoon salt
> ⅛ teaspoon fresh ground pepper
> 1½ pounds calves' brains, cut up
> 3 tablespoons cooking oil or bacon drippings

1. Beat the eggs with the corn meal, salt, and pepper until light. Add the brains, and mix in well.
2. Heat the oil or drippings in a large heavy skillet, add the brains, and cook, stirring, for 10 minutes. Serve hot.

STEWED WILD RABBIT WITH DUMPLINGS

(Makes 8–10 Servings)

> 1 (5 lb.) *wild rabbit, dressed and cut up for stewing*
> *Pepper*
> 1½ *cups flour*
> ¾ *cup cooking oil*
> 2 *quarts water*
> 12 *small white onions, peeled*
> 8 *large carrots, peeled and cut in half*
> 4 *teaspoons salt*

DUMPLINGS:

> 2 *cups flour*
> 1 *tablespoon baking powder*
> ½ *teaspoon salt*
> 1 *tablespoon melted butter or margarine*
> 1 *cup milk*

1. Sprinkle each piece of rabbit well with pepper, then dredge in flour.

2. Place the oil in a large heavy kettle, heat until a drop of water sizzles, then brown each piece of rabbit well on all sides. Transfer to paper toweling to drain. Pour off excess oil from the kettle.

3. Return the rabbit to the kettle, add the water, and simmer, covered, for 2 hours. Add the onions and carrots, cover, and simmer slowly for 1½ hours longer or until vegetables are tender. Stir in the salt.

4. To make the dumplings, sift the dry ingredients together and combine the liquid ingredients. Quickly stir the butter-milk mixture into the flour. Drop dumplings from a spoon into the quickly boiling rabbit gravy. Cover and cook 10 to 12 minutes.

Frogs legs, particularly those of the large bullfrog, were a treasured delicacy among the Plains Indians. Their method of cooking was much the same as ours today: they skinned the legs, broiled them (they used pointed sticks), then salted and ate them. Sometimes the legs were dipped into a batter of wild-fowl eggs and corn meal, then pan-broiled over a crackling fire.

BATTER-FRIED FROGS LEGS

(Makes 4–6 Servings)

> *1 egg, beaten*
> *½ cup corn meal*
> *½ teaspoon salt*
> *⅛ teaspoon fresh ground pepper*
> *2 pounds frogs' legs*
> *½ cup cooking oil*

Mix the egg, corn meal, salt, and pepper together to form a batter. Dip the frogs' legs into the batter, then fry in the oil in a large, heavy skillet for 25 minutes, turning so that they brown evenly on all sides.

Among the lake-country Indians of the northern Plains, particularly the Chippewa and Winnebago, *wild rice* was and still is considered as precious as gold. Invariably, when they venture far from home, a supply of their elegant, long-grain wild rice goes with them, for it can easily be sold at a good price providing necessary money.

GAME HENS WITH WILD RICE-HAZELNUT STUFFING

(Makes 6 Servings)

> *6 frozen Rock Cornish game hens, thawed*
> *Salt and pepper to season*
> *6 tablespoons butter*

STUFFING:

> *1 cup wild rice, washed in cold water*
> *2½ cups water*
> *1 teaspoon salt*
> *4 pieces bacon, cut into julienne strips*
> *5 scallions, washed and sliced (include tops)*
> *½ pound mushrooms, wiped and sliced*
> *1 tablespoon butter or margarine*
> *1 cup raw hazelnuts, halved*
> *Game-hen giblets, chopped*

1. Season hens lightly inside and out with salt and pepper.

2. To prepare stuffing, place wild rice, water, and 1 teaspoon salt in a saucepan, and bring slowly to a boil. Reduce heat, and simmer until all water is

absorbed. Meanwhile, brown bacon in a heavy skillet. Add remaining stuffing ingredients, and sauté, stirring, for 10 minutes. Add wild rice, and toss lightly to mix.

3. Stuff neck and body cavities of each bird, skewer openings shut, and truss.

4. Rub each hen with 1 tablespoon butter or margarine. Place breast side up on a rack in a large, open roasting pan. Wrap any remaining stuffing in aluminum foil, and place in the pan.

5. Roast birds in a moderate oven, 350° F., basting frequently with the drippings, for 2 to 2½ hours or until leg joints move easily. You will have to add more butter for basting from time to time (about ½ cup altogether).

CHIPPEWA WILD RICE

(Makes 4 Servings)

> 1 cup wild rice, washed in cold water
> 2½ cups water
> 1½ teaspoons salt
> 4 strips bacon cut into julienne strips
> 6 eggs
> ¼ teaspoon pepper
> 2 tablespoons minced chives
> Bacon drippings plus melted butter or margarine to
>   measure ⅓ cup

1. Place the wild rice, water, and 1 teaspoon salt in a saucepan, and bring slowly to a boil. Reduce heat and simmer, uncovered, until all water is absorbed.

2. Render the bacon in a large, heavy skillet. Drain bacon on paper toweling. Save drippings.

3. Beat the eggs with ½ teaspoon salt and the pepper until light. Pour into the skillet in which you browned the bacon, and brown the eggs lightly. Then turn gently, as you would a pancake, and brown on the other side. When eggs are firm, cut into julienne strips.

4. Lightly toss the bacon, julienne egg strips, chives, bacon drippings plus melted butter or margarine with the rice. Serve hot as a main dish.

Wild fowl eggs were an important source of protein to Plains Indians, particularly when migrations carried the buffalo far from their lands. At such times women hunted the nests of partridge, quail, duck, and plover and gathered eggs which they would hard-boil, scramble with wild onions, or cook with wild rice. The gatherer approached each nest with reverence, carefully removed the eggs, counted them, adding that number to the total gathered over the years. In that way, each egg representing one year, she could determine how long she had left to live.

EGGS AND WILD ONIONS

(Makes 4 Servings)

5 slices bacon, cut into julienne strips
8 eggs, lightly beaten
½ cup minced scallions or chives
1½ tablespoons minced parsley
1¼ teaspoons salt
¼ teaspoon fresh ground pepper

1. Brown the bacon in a large, heavy skillet.
2. Add eggs, scallions, parsley, salt, and pepper, and scramble gently.
3. Serve at once.

Vegetables

SKILLET CABBAGE

(Makes 6 Servings)

> *6 slices bacon, cut into julienne strips*
> *6 scallions, washed and sliced (include tops)*
> *1 medium-sized cabbage, cut into 8 wedges*
> *¾ cup water*
> *1 teaspoon salt*
> *⅛ teaspoon pepper*

1. Brown the bacon in a large, heavy skillet. Add the scallion, and sauté until golden.

2. Place the cabbage wedges in the skillet; add the water, salt, and pepper; cover, and simmer for 35 minutes, turning occasionally with a fork.

PARCHED CORN

(Makes about 1½ Pints)

2 ears dried corn

Remove the kernels from the cob, place in a very hot iron skillet, cover, and parch, stirring occasionally, for 10 minutes. Serve hot or cold.

CORN OYSTERS

(Makes 6 Servings)

1 (10 oz.) package frozen whole kernel corn
⅔ cup flour
1 teaspoon baking powder
1 teaspoon salt
⅛ teaspoon fresh ground pepper
3 eggs
1 tablespoon honey
¼ cup cooking oil

1. Place the frozen corn in a small saucepan, and cook slowly, without adding any water, for about 10–15 minutes or until the corn is tender.
2. Sift together the dry ingredients. Beat the eggs with the honey until light, and mix into the dry ingredients. Fold in the corn.
3. Heat the oil in a large, heavy skillet until a drop of water will sizzle. Drop the batter from a tablespoon, and brown cakes well on both sides.
4. Serve hot with lots of butter or as pancakes for breakfast with honey or maple syrup.

BAKED POTATOES

(Makes 6 Servings)

>6 Idaho potatoes
>Salt and pepper
>Butter or margarine

1. Scrub potatoes well, then place in a hot oven, 400° F., and bake for about 1 hour or until a fork pierces them easily.

2. Place on a platter and serve accompanied by a large dish of butter, salt and pepper, so that each person can season his potato the way he wants it.

BAKED MUSHROOMS

(Makes 4 Servings)

>¾ pound large mushrooms, wiped with a damp cloth
>¼ cup butter
>½ teaspoon salt
>⅛ teaspoon fresh ground pepper

1. Remove the mushroom stems and slice. Place the mushroom caps, hollow side up, in a large, round pie plate. Lay the sliced stems in and around.

2. Place a generous hunk of butter in the hollow of each mushroom. Sprinkle lightly with salt and pepper.

3. Bake for 30 minutes in a slow oven, 300° F., basting the mushrooms occasionally with the melted butter.

FRIED CUCUMBERS

(Makes 4–6 Servings)

> 4 large cucumbers washed and cut into slices 1/8"
>   thick
> Salt and coarsely ground pepper to season
> Flour for dusting
> Oil or vegetable shortening for frying

1. Spread cucumber slices between layers of paper toweling to dry. Let stand for about an hour.
2. Remove toweling and season slices with salt and pepper.
3. Dip slices in flour and coat both sides lightly.
4. Fry quickly in deep fat until slices are golden brown on each side.
5. Drain on paper toweling and serve at once.

POTATOES BROILED IN BROTH

(Makes 6 Servings)

> 2 pounds new potatoes or other small potatoes,
>   washed
> 6 cups water
> 3 (4.5 gram) packages instant beef broth

Place all ingredients in a large saucepan, and simmer for about 45 minutes or until potatoes are tender. Serve in bowls, topped with some of the broth.

WILD RICE

(Makes 4 Servings)

> 1 cup wild rice, washed in cold water
> 2½ cups water
> 1 teaspoon salt
> Butter or margarine, or bacon or ham drippings to
>   season

1. Place wild rice in a saucepan with the water and salt. Bring slowly to a boil, reduce heat, and simmer, uncovered, until all water is absorbed.

2. Season with butter or margarine, or bacon or ham drippings.

BAKED WILD RICE AND CARROTS

(Makes 6 Servings)

> 1½ cups wild rice, washed in cold water
> 2½ cups water
> 2½ teaspoons salt
> 1 onion, peeled and chopped
> 4 mushrooms, wiped and coarsely chopped
> 4 slices bacon, cut into julienne strips
> 1 cup finely grated carrots
> ½ cup light cream
> 1 egg

1. Place the wild rice, water, and salt in a large saucepan, and bring to a boil. Boil vigorously for about 10 minutes. Turn off heat, cover, and let rice stand for about 20 minutes or until all the water has been absorbed.

2. Brown the bacon, remove from drippings, and drain on paper toweling.

3. Sauté the onions and mushrooms in the bacon drippings until the onions are golden and transparent.

4. Mix the bacon, sautéed onions and mushrooms, and grated carrots into the wild rice.

5. Beat the cream and eggs until light, and fold into the wild-rice mixture.

6. Bake, covered, in a buttered 1½-quart casserole in a moderately slow oven, 325° F., for 30 minutes. Remove cover, stir the mixture well with a fork, and bake for 15 minutes at the same temperature. Stir once again and bake, uncovered, for 15 minutes longer.

Salads

BEET, CUCUMBER, AND ONION SALAD

(Makes 6–8 Servings)

6 medium-sized beets, washed
1 cucumber, washed and sliced
3 yellow onions, peeled and sliced

DRESSING:

¾ cup salad oil
¾ cup cider vinegar

4 teaspoons salt
¼ teaspoon fresh ground pepper

1. Place the beets in a large saucepan, cover with water, and simmer for about 1½ hours or until tender. Peel and slice.

2. Place the sliced beets, cucumbers, and onions in a large bowl, and toss lightly to mix.

3. Mix the dressing ingredients together, dress the salad, toss, and let stand about 1 hour before serving. Toss again and serve.

WILTED SALAD OF MUSTARD GREENS

(Makes 6 Servings)

6 cups washed tender mustard greens (include blossoms, if possible)
4 scallions, washed and sliced thin (include tops)

DRESSING:

8 strips bacon, cut into julienne strips
⅓ cup cider vinegar
1 tablespoon honey
1 teaspoon salt
⅛ teaspoon fresh ground pepper

1. Place the mustard greens and scallions in a large wooden bowl.

2. Brown the bacon, turn off heat, and quickly stir in the vinegar, honey, salt, and pepper.

3. Pour dressing over the greens, and toss well. Let stand about 10 minutes, toss again, and serve.

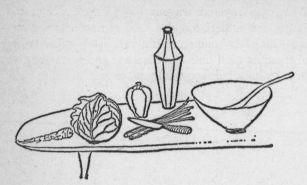

CABBAGE SLAW

(Makes 6 Servings)

½ medium-sized head cabbage, sliced very thin
1 sweet red pepper, washed, cored and chopped
1 carrot, peeled and grated fine
2 scallions, washed and sliced thin

DRESSING:

⅓ cup salad oil
2 tablespoons cider vinegar
1 egg
2 teaspoons salt
⅛ teaspoon fresh ground pepper

1. Place cabbage, sweet red pepper, carrot, and scallions in a large bowl.

2. Beat dressing ingredients together until light, pour over the vegetables, and toss well to mix.

When the covered wagons moved west across the Plains, the settlers found a kind of *nasturtium* growing wild. They named it Indian cress because tribes of the area used both the blossoms and leaves to give their green salads a special pungency.

NASTURTIUM SALAD

(Makes 4 Servings)

DRESSING:

⅓ cup salad oil
¼ cup cider vinegar
1 tablespoon honey
½ teaspoon salt
⅛ teaspoon fresh ground pepper

SALAD:

1 cup young nasturtium leaves, washed
2 cups mixed, prepared salad greens
3 scallions, washed and sliced

1. Combine the dressing ingredients in a shaker jar, and shake to blend. Let stand at room temperature until time to make the salad.

2. Place all salad ingredients in a large wooden bowl, and toss lightly. Dress, toss again, and serve.

SQUAW BREAD

(Makes 3 flat, round loaves, about 10″ in diameter,
½″ thick)

5 cups flour
2 tablespoons baking powder
1 teaspoon salt
1 tablespoon melted butter or margarine
2 cups milk
Cooking oil for frying the bread

1. Sift 4 cups of the flour with the baking powder
and salt.

2. Combine milk and melted margarine or butter.

3. Place flour-baking powder mixture in a large
bowl, and add the liquid ingredients, a little at a time,
beating them in at first with an egg beater.

4. When the 4 cups have been worked into a soft
dough with the milk, lightly flour a board with part
of the remaining 1 cup of flour. Turn the dough out
onto the board, and knead lightly, working in the
rest of the flour.

5. Divide the dough into three parts, and shape
each into a round pone about ⅛″ thick and a diameter
to fit the skillet you plan to fry the bread in.

6. Pour enough cooking oil into a large, heavy
skillet to measure about ¼″ deep.

7. Heat the oil, and brown the breads quickly,
one at a time, until golden on both sides.

8. Spread with any meat mixture or jam or stewed
dry fruits. Cut into wedges and serve at once.

CHIPPEWA BANNOCK

(Makes 6 Servings)

> 2 cups flour
> ½ teaspoon salt
> 1 teaspoon baking powder
> 5 tablespoons bacon drippings
> ¾ cup water
> ¼ cup cooking oil

1. Sift together the dry ingredients, then mix in the bacon drippings and water.

2. Heat the oil in a large, heavy skillet until a drop of water sizzles. Drop the batter from a teaspoon, flatten into cakes, and cook 3 to 5 minutes on a side or until well browned. Serve hot or cold.

POPCORN

(Makes about 2 Quarts)

> ⅓ cup cooking oil
> ½ cup popcorn
> ¼ cup melted butter or margarine
> Salt to season

1. Heat the oil in a large saucepan until a kernel of corn sizzles when dropped in. Add the corn, cover with a tight-fitting lid, and heat, shaking the pan, until all corn has popped.

2. Pour into a bowl, top with melted butter or margarine, sprinkle with salt, and toss well.

WILD RICE JOHNNY CAKES

(Makes about 6 Cakes)

> 1 cup wild rice, washed in cold water
> 3 cups water
> 1 teaspoon salt
> 3 tablespoons white corn meal
> Bacon drippings

1. Place the wild rice, water, and salt in a saucepan, bring to a boil, and boil gently, uncovered, for about 35 minutes or until the rice is tender but not mushy.

2. Stir in the corn meal, a tablespoon at a time. Let mixture cool until it can be shaped with the hands. Shape into flat cakes about 2½ to 3 inches in diameter.

3. Brown well on both sides in bacon drippings, and drain on paper toweling. Eat hot or cold.

Desserts

For centuries, *pemmican* was a staple among the Plains Indians, and a nourishing food it was. Wherever hunters roamed, they carried supplies of this early K-ration in leather pouches. Whole tribes ate it during winter months, when other foods were scarce. The original recipe, a forerunner of mincemeat as we know it today, was a mixture of lean beef or venison, dried and pounded to powder, melted fat, and acid berries, most probably buffalo berries. Later, with the arrival of spices and apples, the recipe was refined and emerged as a piquant filling for fritters, turnovers, and pies.

VENISON MINCEMEAT

(Makes 2 Quarts)

1 quart apple cider
2 cups seedless raisins
1 cup dried currants
3 greening apples, peeled, cored and chopped
1 cup chopped suet
2 pounds ground venison
2 teaspoons salt
2 teaspoons cinnamon
2 teaspoons ginger
1 teaspoon cloves
1 teaspoon nutmeg
½ teaspoon allspice

1. Place the cider, raisins, currants, apples, and suet in a large, heavy kettle, cover, and simmer for 2 hours.

2. Stir in remaining ingredients, and simmer, uncovered, for 2 hours, stirring occasionally. Use as pie filling.

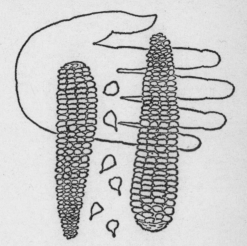

THE PLANTERS OF THE SOUTH

THE PLANTERS OF THE SOUTH

It was through the West Indies and the southern Atlantic states that Europeans were first introduced to North America and its strange new foods. Columbus, who found the natives "no wild savages, but very gentile and courteous," was welcomed with a feast of broiled fresh fish, custard apples, baked yams, a bread of cassavas, and succulent, sweet guavas.

When Spanish adventurers arrived years later, they found oysters, shrimp, and blue crabs blown onto the beaches by sub-tropical storms. They discovered coastal waters teaming with flounder and whitefish and drum; clear mountain streams swarming with trout; forests full of squirrels, rabbits, opossums, deer, and bear. Salt marshes echoed the cries of cranes and ospreys; fields rustled with quail, plover, and pheasant. The soil, too, was fertile and well watered by the streams rippling through it. In this land of plenty, the Spaniards first saw southern Indian tribes growing acres of pumpkins, squash, and corn, with beans climbing the stalks. The woodlands were filled with hickory nuts and pecans, blackberries, wild strawberries, persimmons, and a fragrant plant called the spicebush, which Indian women used for seasoning. There were sassafras, wild mint, and yaupon, which were steeped into teas.

When John Smith first arrived at Jamestown, he met with an "abundance of fish, lying so thicke with their heads above the water, as for want of nets (our barge driving amongst them) we attempted to catch them with a frying-pan . . . neither better fish, more plentie, nor more varitie for small fish, had any of us ever seene in any place so swimming in the water." He found so many sting rays along the shore that he amused himself by nailing them to the ground with his sword. "We tooke more in owne houre than we could eate in a day," he wrote. Inland he talked of "great heapes of corn" and of Indians who brought him "venison, turkies, wild fowle, bread and what else they had." The Nansamonds brought him four hundred baskets of corn, and the Chickahominies, though they complained of few staples, "fraughted him" with another hundred bushels.

During the winter of 1607–8 he wrote that "the rivers became so covered with swans, geese, ducks and cranes, that we daily feasted with good bread, Virginia pease, pumpions and putchamins (persimmons), fish, fowle and diverse sorts of wild beasts, so fat as we could eate them."

The Jamestown colonists spent their first Christmas among the Powhatans, and of this Smith said, "And we were never more merry nor fed on more plenty of good oysters, fish, flesh, wild fowle and good bread nor ever had better fires in England."

Had it not been for their Indian friends, the English would have died of starvation their first winter in Virginia. When their own crops failed, Indian women showed them how to gather persimmons after the first frost had removed their astringency and to mash them into a paste for puddings and cakes. They brought the white women corn and taught them to pound it into meal and make breads and puddings of it.

In Florida, the Spanish fared equally as well. The Creeks and Seminoles showed them how to pound the hickory nut and take a sweet milk from the meal for enriching soups; how to wrap fresh fish with grapes and steam them in fragrant leaves. The Choctaws taught them to grind sassafras leaves into a powder that would both thicken and sweeten the broth of stews.

It was the Spaniards who introduced the orange, and the Indians of Florida and the Gulf Coast quickly learned to cook it with fish. Years later, when the naturalist William Bartram traveled among the Seminole, he described two dishes they served him: a red snapper that had been steamed with fresh oranges; and whole oranges, cut and marinated in honey for several days, that were served as dessert. He wrote also of the honeyed drink the Indians prepared and of a cream made from hickory nuts.

"The Creeks store up shell-barked hiccory nuts in their towns," he said. "I have seen above an hundred bushels of these nuts belonging to one family. They pound them into pieces, then cast them into boiling water, which, after passing through fine strainers, preserves the most oily part of the liquid: they call this by a name which signifies hiccory milk; it is as sweet and rich as fresh cream, and is an ingredient in most of their cookery, especially homony and corn cakes."

Of interest, too, is a Creek feast that Bartram attended: "The repast is now brought in, consisting of venison stewed with bear's oil, fresh corn cakes, milk and homony; and our drink, honey and water, very cool and agreeable."

He was later invited to a Seminole feast of which he wrote: "The ribs and choicest fat pieces of the bullocks, excellently well barbecued, were brought into the apartment of the public square, constructed and appointed for feasting; bowls and kettles of stewed fish and broth were brought in for the next course, and with it a very singular dish, the traders call it tripe soup."

The Cherokee of northern Georgia and later

North Carolina were among the more advanced Indian tribes. A Cherokee named Sequoyah studied the characters of the Roman alphabet and devised a Cherokee alphabet of eighty-six symbols which is still used today on the Cherokee Reservation of North Carolina.

Cherokee women were excellent cooks. They took green beans from the fields, strung and sun-dried them into Leather Britches Beans. They concocted delicious stews of venison, squirrel and rabbit; and made puddings of wild persimmons; and a bread of dried beans and corn meal.

The Museum of the Cherokee Indian at Cherokee, North Carolina, now sponsors an annual feast of Cherokee foods. The menu of the second feast, held in 1949, is typical and though prodigiously long, worth our noting. It included: parched corn, blackberries, huckleberries, wild strawberries, raspberries, elderberries, wild plums, crab apples, ground cherries, persimmons, field apricots, fall grapes, fox grapes, opossum grapes, dewberries, gooseberries, hickory nuts, hazelnuts, walnuts, butternuts, a drink called sumacade, sassafras tea, spicewood tea, chestnut bread, bean bread, hominy bread, wild-potato bread, sweet-potato bread, molasses bread, roast deer, broiled speckled trout, roast bison, sautéed mushrooms, stewed raccoon, roast turkey, boiled potatoes, roasted corn, hominy, beans cooked with fat back, wild greens, pumpkin, succotash, boiled Jerusalem artichokes, and ramps!

These are all Indian foods and substantial contributions to today's southern diet. Women of the Cherokee, Choctaw, Seminole, Powhatan, Creek, and other tribes developed hundreds of recipes, many of which are American favorites today. They created succotash, Brunswick stew, corn pone, hominy and hominy grits, roasted peanuts, fried green tomatoes, a stew of fresh shrimp and okra, to name only a few.

You'll find these recipes on the following pages as well as a good many more that we now consider favorites. They prove that the southern Indians' addition to the world's menu is varied, creative, and that it lives still, little changed.

Appetizers

Jerusalem artichokes, unlike the prickly globe, or French, artichokes, are knobby tubers. They grew wild throughout the South and were much relished by Indians living there. Eaten raw, Jerusalem artichokes are as crisp and succulent as a radish; cooked, they have the flavor and texture of an Irish potato, though not quite so starchy.

JERUSALEM ARTICHOKES AS AN APPETIZER

(Makes 6–8 Servings)

> *1 pound Jerusalem artichokes*
> *Salt and pepper to season*

1. Wash the Jerusalem artichokes well and crispen in ice water.
2. Sprinkle with salt and pepper to season.
3. Eat out of the hand as you would radishes.

Peanuts were probably the most versatile and nourishing of the foods that grew wild throughout the South. In lean months, the Indians used them as a meat substitute by brewing them into thick soups and stews. And they enjoyed them as we do today, roasted and salted. The sea was the Indian's supply of salt, and by boiling a gallon or so of sea water they were able to produce crystalline salt.

FRESH ROASTED PEANUTS

(Makes 2 Pounds)

> 2 pounds blanched green peanuts
> ¼ cup butter or margarine
> Salt to season

1. Place peanuts and butter or margarine in a large, shallow baking pan, and roast in a slow oven, 300°F., for 2 hours, stirring frequently.
2. Remove from oven, drain on paper toweling, and sprinkle with salt to taste.

Soups

PEANUT SOUP

(Makes 6 Servings)

> 1 (9½ oz.) jar dry roasted peanuts
> 2 cups milk
> 2 cups water
> 2 (5.4 gram) packages instant chicken broth
> 1 tablespoon minced chives

Chop the nuts fine, or purée in a blender. Place the nuts and the remaining ingredients in a large saucepan, and heat, stirring, for 15 to 20 minutes. Serve hot. Make the portions small—the soup is rich.

JERUSALEM ARTICHOKE SOUP

(Makes 6–8 Servings)

1 pound Jerusalem artichokes, carefully washed
2 scallions, washed and sliced
2 (5.4 gram) packages instant chicken broth
6 cups water
2 teaspoons salt
⅛ teaspoon pepper
2 eggs, lightly beaten

1. Parboil the Jerusalem artichokes for 20 to 25 minutes until tender. Drain and slice the artichokes in half. Scoop the flesh away from the skins, pressing it out of the small, knobby portions. Mash the artichokes until smooth.

2. Place the mashed artichokes, scallions, instant chicken broth, water, salt, and pepper in a large saucepan, and simmer together for 15 minutes.

3. Pour a little of the hot soup into the beaten eggs, stirring vigorously. Then return the egg mixture to the soup, stirring and heating for about 1 minute. Serve at once.

Indians discovered early the special properties of ashes mixed with water. They knew that corn soaked in such a mixture became puffed and white and of a different flavor altogether. It was, of course, *hominy* which the Indian women fermented into a sour soup, fried in a skillet with meat and wild greens, or baked into a custardy pudding. Some hominy was dried and pounded into grits which were also eaten with relish. Most often, grits were boiled with water to make a simple gruel. Any leftovers were set out to harden so that they could then be sliced and fried in oil.

HOMINY SOUP

(Makes 8–10 Servings)

> ¼ pound salt pork, sliced about ¼" thick
> 1 medium yellow onion, peeled and sliced thin
> 2 (1 lb. 13 oz.) cans hominy, drained
> 1 quart buttermilk
> ½ teaspoon salt
> ¼ teaspoon fresh ground pepper

1. Render the salt pork thoroughly in a large, heavy kettle. Drain off drippings.

2. Add onion to the kettle, and sauté slowly until golden and transparent.

3. Mix in the hominy, and heat gently, stirring, for about 5 minutes.

4. Add buttermilk, salt, and pepper, and heat very slowly (do not allow to simmer) for about 5 minutes. This soup should be served warm, not hot.

Main Dishes

SHRIMP AND OKRA SOUP

(Makes 6–8 Servings)

> 1 pound okra, washed
> 6 tomatoes, washed and cored
> 1 bay leaf, crumbled
> 4 peppercorns
> 1 cup water
> 1½ pounds shelled and deveined raw shrimp
> ½ teaspoon gumbo filé mixed with 1 tablespoon cold water
> 1½ teaspoons salt

1. Leave the small okra pods whole, but slice the larger ones in two crosswise.

2. Place the okra, tomatoes, bay leaf, peppercorns, and water in a large, heavy kettle, and simmer, covered, for 20 minutes, or until the tomatoes have broken up and the okra is tender.

3. Add the shrimp, and simmer 10 minutes more. Stir in the gumbo filé and salt, and simmer for about 10 minutes. Serve hot in soup bowls.

BROILED SHRIMP

(Makes 6–8 Servings)

4½ pounds fresh shrimp in the shell
1¾ cups water
4 cloves garlic, peeled and crushed
½ cup cooking oil
¼ teaspoon orégano
1 teaspoon salt

1. Place the shrimp in a large kettle, add water, cover, and bring slowly to a simmer. Steam the shrimp for 20 minutes, then drain, reserving 1 cup of their broth.

2. Mix together the garlic, cooking oil, orégano, and salt.

3. Shell and devein shrimp. Place on a broiler

pan, pour the garlic-oil mixture over the shrimp, and broil for 5 minutes.

4. Turn the shrimp, pour shrimp broth over them, and broil about 2 minutes longer, basting with the broth. Top each serving with a little of the broth.

Women of the Deep South tribes, such as the Creek and Seminole, were accustomed to serving *fresh fish and fruit* at the same meal. Soon they were putting the two together, steaming fish with oranges or wild grapes to produce dishes that were more succulent and flavorful than ever.

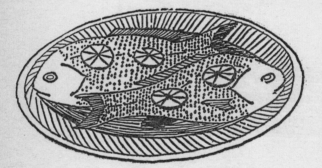

RED SNAPPER BAKED WITH ORANGES

(Makes 6–8 Servings)

    2 (2 lb.) red snappers, cleaned
    2 tablespoons butter
    ½ cup chopped parsley
    ⅛ teaspoon fresh ground pepper
    4 oranges, washed and sliced

1. Place the fish in a large baking pan. Dot each well with butter, and sprinkle with parsley and pepper. Lay the orange slices over the fish.

2. Bake in a hot oven, 400° F., for 20 minutes. Reduce heat to moderate, 350° F., and bake for 20 minutes more or until fish flakes at the touch of a fork.

BOILED BLUE CRABS

(Makes 4–6 Servings)

12 live hard-shell crabs
Melted butter

1. Plunge the crabs into a large kettle of rapidly boiling water, and boil, covered, for 25 minutes.

2. Set a steaming platter of crabs on the table, and supply each person with crackers for cracking the shell, and an individual ramekin of melted butter. Only the meat on the under side of the shell and that of the claws is succulent and sweet. Avoid spongy or feathery portions. The tamale, or green liver, however, is delicious.

TURKEY WITH OYSTER-CORNBREAD STUFFING

(Makes 6–8 Servings)

TURKEY:

1 (8 lb.) turkey
1½ cups water
1 cup butter or margarine, softened

STUFFING:

8 cups crumbled cornbread or muffins
5 scallions, washed and minced (include tops)
10 medium sized mushrooms, wiped and chopped
1 cup coarsely chopped pecans
18 oysters, drained and chopped (reserve liquid)
Turkey giblets, cooked and chopped
1 egg
1 clove garlic, peeled and crushed
2 tablespoons minced parsley
½ teaspoon powdered savory
¼ teaspoon fresh ground pepper
2½ teaspoons salt
5 tablespoons oyster liquid
5 tablespoons giblet-cooking water
¼ cup melted butter or margarine

1. Wipe turkey well with a damp cloth inside and out. Remove any pinfeathers, and singe off hairs.

2. Simmer the giblets in 1½ cups water for 20 to 30 minutes. Remove from cooking water, and chop. Save the cooking water.

3. Mix the dressing ingredients together thoroughly, and stuff both neck and body cavities of the bird. Wrap remaining stuffing in aluminum foil. Skewer the openings shut, truss, and place the turkey breast down on a poultry rack in a large roasting pan. Place the foil-wrapped stuffing in the bottom of the pan. Rub the bird generously with about ¼ cup of the softened butter.

4. Roast the turkey, uncovered, in a moderately slow oven, 325° F., basting every 20 minutes with a mixture of the oyster liquid, giblet-cooking water, and remaining butter, melted. After 1½ hours of roasting, turn the turkey breast side up. Allow about 30 minutes per pound for roasting the turkey. The turkey is done when the leg joint moves easily.

POMPANO STEAMED WITH GRAPES

(Makes 4–6 Servings)

4 (1 lb.) pompanos, cleaned
1 pound scuppernong, muscadine, or other grapes, washed and seeded
2 tablespoons butter or margarine
Salt and pepper to season

1. Place fish on a large piece of heavy aluminum foil in a baking pan.

2. Inside each fish place a small lump of butter and 4 grapes.

3. Dot the fish well with butter, and arrange grapes on top.

4. Cover with a second large piece of aluminum foil, and seal the edges of the two.

5. Place in a hot oven, 400° F., and let steam for 30 minutes. Loosen the top piece of foil, salt and pepper the fish, and baste with the drippings. Reseal and steam for 15 minutes longer.

6. Baste once more with the drippings, and serve.

Women of the Powhatan, Chickahominy, and Cherokee kept a kettle of *soup* or *stew* bubbling at all times. It was their way of using up leftovers. A particular favorite was a mixture of game or fowl, usually squirrel, rabbit, or turkey, corn, beans, and tomatoes, which the Jamestown settlers called Brunswick Stew.

BRUNSWICK STEW

(Makes 12–14 Servings)

    1 (5 lb.) chicken
    Water for stewing
    2 bay leaves, crumbled
    5 peppercorns
    3 sprigs parsley
    1 stalk celery
    2 potatoes, peeled and cut in ½" cubes
    2 large onions, peeled and quartered
    2 (10 oz.) packages frozen kernel corn
    2 (10 oz.) packages frozen baby Lima beans

2 tablespoons salt
¼ teaspoon coarsely ground pepper
½ teaspoon orégano
Pinch mace
6 tomatoes, washed, cored and quartered

1. Place the chicken, neck, and giblets in a large, heavy kettle. Add just enough water to cover, the bay leaves, peppercorns, parsley sprigs, and celery stalk, and simmer slowly, covered, for about 1½ to 2 hours or until the meat is tender and will easily separate from the bones.

2. Remove chicken from the pot, separate meat from the bones, and return meat to the broth.

3. Add all remaining ingredients except tomatoes, and simmer about 30 minutes or until vegetables are tender.

4. Add tomatoes and simmer about 10 minutes more. Serve at once.

CHICKEN BAKED WITH SCALLIONS, MUSHROOMS, AND TOMATOES

(Makes 4–6 Servings)

1 (2½ lb.) frying chicken, cut up
Salt and fresh ground pepper to season
12 whole scallions (include about 2" of the top)
16 medium mushroom caps, wiped with a damp cloth
3 tomatoes, washed, cored, and quartered
2 tablespoons fresh minced dill
2 tablespoons butter or margarine

1. Salt and pepper each piece of chicken lightly. Place about half of the chicken in the bottom of a 2-quart baking dish (one with a close-fitting lid). Arrange 6 scallions, 8 mushroom caps, and 4 tomato quarters in

143

and around the chicken. Sprinkle lightly with salt, fresh ground pepper, and 1 tablespoon minced dill. Dot all with 1 tablespoon butter or margarine.

2. Lay remaining pieces of chicken on top, placing remaining scallions and mushroom caps in and around. Sprinkle with salt and pepper and minced dill. Dot with remaining butter or margarine.

3. Top with remaining tomato quarters, pushing them down, if necessary, to make the lid fit tightly.

4. Bake, covered, for 2 hours in a slow oven, 300°F. Remove from oven, stir well, mashing tomatoes into the juices.

5. Return to a moderate oven, 350° F., and bake, uncovered, for 2 hours more. Serve chicken topped with vegetables and sauce.

Vegetables

One of the first Indian recipes adopted by the colonists was a mixture of boiled beans and corn sweetened with the fat of the bear. The natives called it *m'sickquotash*, but to the English it became simply *succotash*.

SUCCOTASH

(Makes 4–6 Servings)

⅓ cup julienne strips of pork jowl or bacon
1 onion, peeled and coarsely chopped
⅓ cup chopped green pepper
1 (10 oz.) package frozen baby Lima beans
1 (10 oz.) package frozen kernel corn
1 cup water
2 tablespoons butter or margarine
Salt and fresh ground black pepper to season

1. Slowly render the pork jowl or bacon in a large, heavy skillet.

2. Add onion and green pepper, and sauté until onion is golden.

3. Add frozen beans, corn, and the water, and simmer, covered, until vegetables are tender, about 15 minutes.

4. Season with butter or margarine and salt and black pepper to taste.

BAKED SWEET POTATOES

(Makes 6 Servings)

> *6 medium sweet potatoes*
> *Butter*
> *Honey*

1. Wash the potatoes well, and bake in a hot oven, 400°F., for about 1 hour or until tender.

2. Serve with butter and honey.

SWEET POTATO CAKES

(Makes 10–12 Servings)

> *4 large sweet potatoes*
> *3 eggs*
> *1 cup flour*
> *1½ teaspoons salt*
> *⅛ teaspoon fresh ground pepper*
> *2 tablespoons cooking oil*

1. Parboil the potatoes until tender; peel and mash them.

2. Mix in the eggs, flour, salt, and pepper. Heat the oil on a large griddle until a drop of water sizzles. Drop the potato batter from a large spoon, and brown on both sides. As you turn the pancakes, flatten them with a spatula slightly. Add more oil to the griddle as needed. This recipe will make about 15 cakes about 3″ in diameter. Serve hot with butter and, if you like, honey.

BEAN CAKES

(Makes 10–12 Servings)

½ pound pea beans, washed, soaked, and cooked by package directions
1 cup corn meal
1 cup flour
2 teaspoons salt
1 teaspoon baking powder
⅛ teaspoon fresh ground pepper
1 cup milk
2 eggs, lightly beaten
2 tablespoons cooking oil

1. Drain the beans thoroughly, and cool to room temperature.

2. Sift together the corn meal, flour, salt, baking powder, and pepper. Mix together the milk and eggs, and then stir them into the sifted dry ingredients.

3. Fold in the beans. Heat the oil in a large, heavy skillet until a drop of water sizzles. Drop the bean batter from a tablespoon, and brown cakes on both sides.

4. Serve hot as a substitute for potatoes, with lots of butter.

ROASTING EARS

(Makes 4–6 Servings)

> 6 ears sweet corn in the husk
> 6 quarts water
> 6 tablespoons salt

1. Peel off the outer husks only and pull out tassels.

2. Mix water and salt in a large deep kettle. Submerge corn in the salt water, weight down, and soak for 1 hour.

3. Remove ears from salt water, wrap tightly in aluminum foil.

4. Roast in a hot oven, 400°F., for 1½ hours.

5. Unwrap, and serve with butter, salt, and pepper.

FRIED HOMINY

(Makes 6–8 Servings)

> 6 strips bacon, cut into julienne pieces
> 2 (1 lb.) cans hominy, drained
> ⅛ teaspoon fresh ground pepper
> 2 scallions, washed and sliced thin (include tops)
> ½ teaspoon salt

1. Render the bacon in a large, heavy skillet until brown and crisp.

2. Stir in hominy and sauté, stirring, for 5 minutes.

3. Add pepper, scallions, and salt, and sauté, stirring, for 5 minutes more.

BAKED HOMINY

(Makes 6 Servings)

2 (1 lb.) cans hominy
4 tablespoons butter
4 eggs, lightly beaten
2 teaspoons salt
⅛ teaspoon fresh ground pepper

1. Drain the hominy well, reserving the liquid. There should be about 1⅓ cups. If not, add enough water to bring the measure to 1⅓ cups.

2. Heat the hominy liquid with the butter just until the butter is melted. Slowly pour the liquid into the eggs, stirring constantly. Add the salt and pepper to the egg mixture.

3. Pour the egg mixture over the hominy, stir to mix, then pour into a 2-quart baking dish. Set the dish in a pan of cold water, place in a moderate oven, 350°F., and bake for 1 hour. Serve piping hot.

BAKED CUCUMBERS

(Makes 4–6 Servings)

4 cucumbers, peeled and quartered lengthwise
2 tablespoons butter or margarine
1 teaspoon salt
1 teaspoon dill seed, crushed
¼ teaspoon fresh ground pepper

1. Place a layer of cucumbers in the bottom of an 8″ × 8″ × 2″ baking dish and dot with half of the butter or margarine.

2. Mix together the seasonings, and sprinkle half over the layer of cucumbers.

3. Add a second layer of cucumbers, dot with butter, and sprinkle with remaining seasonings.

4. Bake, uncovered, in a hot oven, 400°F., for 1 hour. Stir cucumbers lightly once, pushing the top layer to the bottom and lifting the bottom cucumbers to the top. Serve hot.

BAKED ACORN SQUASH

(Makes 8 Servings)

4 medium-sized acorn squash
16 teaspoons honey
8 tablespoons butter or margarine
Fresh ground pepper to season

1. Slice the squash in half crosswise and scoop out the pulp and seeds. Trim the bottoms, if necessary, so that the squash will stand hollow side up.

2. Place 2 teaspoons honey in the hollow of each squash, then add 1 tablespoon butter or margarine to each and a twist or two of fresh ground pepper.

3. Place squash in a large, shallow baking pan and bake, uncovered, in a moderate oven, 350°F., for about 2½ hours or until the squash are tender.

BAKED SQUASH AND WILD ONIONS

(Makes 4–6 Servings)

> 2 pounds yellow squash or zucchini, washed and
>   sliced crosswise ¼" thick
> 8 scallions, washed and sliced crosswise ¼" thick
>   (include some tops)
> ½ teaspoon dill seed, crushed
> 1 teaspoon salt
> ¼ teaspoon marjoram
> ¼ teaspoon fresh ground pepper
> 3 tablespoons butter or margarine

1. Place squash in an 8" × 8" × 2" baking dish; add scallions, distributing them well.

2. Mix together the seasonings, and sprinkle over all. Dot squash with butter.

3. Cover dish with aluminum foil, and bake in a moderate oven, 350°F., for 2½ hours.

GREEN BEANS WITH FAT BACK

(Makes 4–6 Servings)

> 1 pound fresh green beans
> 1½ quarts water
> 2 (2") cubes fat back or salt pork
> Salt to season
> Fresh ground pepper to season

1. Wash the beans well, snap off ends, and remove strings.

2. Place beans, water, and fat back or salt pork in a large, heavy saucepan, and simmer very slowly, uncovered, for 4 hours.

3. Season to taste with salt and pepper, and serve.

SKILLET CORN

(Makes 4 Servings)

>   4 strips bacon, cut into julienne pieces
>   6 ears sweet corn
>   4 scallions, washed and sliced thin (include tops)
>   1 tablespoon fresh minced dill
>   ½ teaspoon salt
>   ⅛ teaspoon fresh ground pepper
>   1½ cups water

1. Brown the bacon slowly. Meanwhile, cut the kernels from the cob; also scrape away the pulp and milk.

2. Add kernels, pulp, and milk to bacon and drippings. Stir in the scallions, dill, salt, and pepper. Sauté, stirring, for 15 minutes.

3. Add the water, and simmer slowly for 1 hour.

FRIED GREEN TOMATOES

(Makes 6 Servings)

>   2 pounds green tomatoes, washed
>   4 eggs
>   1¼ cups corn meal
>   ¾ cup water
>   ¼ cup minced chives
>   1 tablespoon salt
>   ¼ teaspoon fresh ground pepper
>   ¼ cup butter or margarine

1. Slice the tomatoes ½" thick (do not peel or core). Drain well between several thicknesses of paper

toweling until most of the moisture of the tomatoes is absorbed.

2. While the tomatoes are draining, make a batter by beating the eggs until light, then mixing in the corn meal, water, minced chives, salt, and pepper.

3. In a large, heavy iron skillet, heat the butter or margarine until bubbly.

4. Dip tomato slices into batter, and brown quickly on both sides. Serve at once.

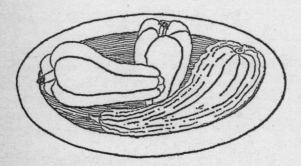

BAKED SWEET RED PEPPERS AND YELLOW SQUASH

(Makes 4–6 Servings)

2 pounds yellow squash, washed and sliced ¼" thick
2 sweet red peppers, washed and cut into pieces about 1" × 1"
2 tomatoes, washed and sliced ¼" thick
6 scallions, washed and sliced ¼" thick (include tops)
1 clove garlic, peeled and crushed
½ teaspoon crushed dill seed
½ teaspoon crushed coriander seed
1 teaspoon salt
⅛ teaspoon fresh ground black pepper
3 tablespoons butter or margarine

1. Place all vegetables in a 9″ × 13″ × 2″ baking pan, sprinkle with the seasonings, and dot with butter.

2. Toss all together lightly as you would a salad to mix.

3. Cover pan tightly with aluminum foil and let stand at room temperature about 3 hours before baking.

4. Bake in a moderate oven, 350°F., for 3 hours.

JERUSALEM ARTICHOKES BAKED IN HOT ASHES

(Makes 6 Servings)

1 pound Jerusalem artichokes
Butter to season
Salt and pepper to season

1. Wash the artichokes well, wrap in heavy aluminum foil—wrap each artichoke individually.

2. Place in glowing coals. Charcoal briquettes prepared for broiling meat work well.

3. Roast for 8 minutes; turn and roast for 8 minutes more.

4. Serve hot, as a potato substitute, with lots of butter, salt, and pepper.

JERUSALEM ARTICHOKES SAUTÉED IN OIL AND VINEGAR

(Makes 6 Servings)

1 pound Jerusalem artichokes
½ cup salad oil

2 tablespoons minced chives
2 tablespoons minced fresh dill
½ teaspoon salt
⅛ teaspoon fresh ground pepper
¼ cup vinegar

1. Wash the artichokes well, and parboil for 20 minutes. Drain.

2. Place the artichokes in a large, heavy skillet along with the oil, chives, and dill. Season with salt and pepper. Sauté, stirring, for 15 minutes.

3. Add the vinegar, and simmer for 5 minutes longer. Serve as a hot salad.

LEATHER BRITCHES BEANS

(Makes 4–6 Servings)
NOTE: This recipe takes two months to prepare

1 pound green beans, washed
2 quarts water
¼ pound salt pork, diced
2 teaspoons salt
⅛ teaspoon fresh ground pepper

1. Snap the ends off the beans, and string on heavy thread. Hang in a sunny place to dry for two months.

2. When you are ready to cook the beans, soak them for 1 hour in the two quarts water.

3. Add the salt pork, salt, and pepper, and bring to a boil. Reduce heat, and simmer very slowly, stirring occasionally, for 3 hours. Add additional water if necessary. Serve hot, with lots of broth, as a vegetable. Corn Pone* is the perfect accompaniment—good for "sopping up" the potlikker.

HOT TURNIP GREENS SALAD

(Makes 4 Servings)

> 2 pounds fresh turnip greens
> 2½ quarts water
> 1 tablespoon salt
> ½ cup diced salt pork or sow belly
> ⅓ cup cider vinegar
> Pinch fresh ground pepper

1. Wash turnip greens well and remove coarse stems. Place in a large saucepan; add water and salt. Bring to a boil, reduce heat, cover, and simmer 20 minutes.

2. Meanwhile, render the salt pork in a skillet. Mix in the vinegar and pepper.

3. Drain cooked greens well, place in a large salad bowl, top with sizzling vinegar-and-salt-pork mixture, toss lightly, and serve at once.

JERUSALEM ARTICHOKE SALAD

(Makes 6 Servings)

> 1 pound Jerusalem artichokes, washed and diced
> ½ cup salad oil
> ⅓ cup cider vinegar
> 1 tablespoon minced scallions
> 1 tablespoon honey
> ½ teaspoon salt
> ⅛ teaspoon fresh ground pepper

1. Place the diced Jerusalem artichokes in a large wooden bowl.

2. Mix the oil, vinegar, scallions, honey, salt, and pepper, and dress the artichokes.

3. Toss to mix. Let marinate at room temperature for 1 hour. Toss again and serve.

SMOTHERED GREENS

(Makes 6 Servings)

5 strips bacon, cut into julienne strips
3 scallions, washed and sliced (include tops)
⅓ cup vinegar
1 tablespoon honey
½ teaspoon salt
⅛ teaspoon fresh ground pepper
2 quarts greens, washed and prepared for salad

1. Render the bacon in a heavy skillet until crisp and brown. Add the scallions, and sauté, stirring, for about 5 minutes.

2. Stir in the vinegar, honey, salt, and pepper, and heat, stirring, for 5 minutes.

3. Place the greens in a wooden salad bowl, pour the hot dressing over all, toss, and serve.

HEARTS OF PALM SALAD

(Makes 4 Servings)

   2 (*14 oz.*) *cans hearts of palm, drained*

DRESSING:

   2 *tablespoons finely minced scallions*
   ¼ *cup salad oil*
   3 *tablespoons cider vinegar*
   1 *teaspoon salt*
   1 *teaspoon paprika*
   ⅛ *teaspoon fresh ground pepper*

   1. Cut the hearts of palm into thin strips and arrange on a small, flat platter.
   2. Mix together all dressing ingredients, and spread over the hearts of palm.
   3. Let the salad marinate at room temperature for about 30 minutes before serving.

Breads

HOMINY GRITS

(Makes 6 Servings)

   1 *cup hominy grits*
   5 *cups water*
   1¼ *teaspoons salt*
   Butter
   Fresh ground pepper

1. Bring the water to a rapid boil and gradually add the hominy grits, stirring continually. Season with salt, and boil the mixture gently, stirring occasionally, for 20 minutes.

2. Remove from heat, spoon into bowls, and season with lots of butter and a sprinkling of fresh ground pepper.

FRIED HOMINY GRITS

(Makes about 8 Servings)

1 recipe Hominy Grits*
⅓ cup bacon drippings

1. Spoon the grits into glasses, and chill overnight.

2. Unmold, slice into rounds about ½ inch thick, and brown on both sides in bacon drippings.

CARROT BREAD

(Makes 8–10 Servings)

1 pound carrots, peeled and grated
¾ cup water
1 cup corn meal
1½ cups flour
1 teaspoon baking powder
1½ teaspoons salt
2 tablespoons sugar
2 tablespoons melted butter
1¼ cups warm milk
2 tablespoons molasses
2 eggs, lightly beaten

1. Simmer the grated carrots in the water, covered, for 15 minutes. Place in a sieve and set aside to drain.

2. Sift together the corn meal, flour, baking powder, salt, and sugar, and place in a mixing bowl.

3. Combine the butter, milk, molasses, and eggs, and mix into the dry ingredients.

4. Using a wooden spoon, press all water from the carrots and fold them into the batter.

5. Pour into a well-greased 8″×8″×2″ baking dish and bake in a hot oven, 400°F., for 1 hour.

6. Cut into large squares and serve hot with lots of butter. This is a bread to be eaten with a fork.

SWEET POTATO BREAD

(Makes 8–10 Servings)

> 2 large sweet potatoes
> 1 cup corn meal
> 1 cup flour
> 1 teaspoon baking powder
> 1½ teaspoons salt
> 2 tablespoons honey
> 2 tablespoons melted butter
> 1¼ cups warm milk
> 2 eggs, lightly beaten

1. Parboil the sweet potatoes for about 50 minutes or until just tender. Cool, peel, and cut into ¼″ cubes.

2. Sift together the dry ingredients and place in a mixing bowl. Combine the honey, butter, milk, and eggs, and mix into the dry ingredients.

3. Fold in the cubed sweet potatoes, pour batter into a well-greased 8″×8″×2″ baking dish, and bake in a hot oven, 400°F., for 1 hour.

4. Cut into large squares and serve hot with lots of butter. This is a bread to be eaten with a fork.

Pones, or flattened cakes of corn meal and water, were the basic, everyday breads of southern tribes. Usually they were baked on wooden paddles in the fire or tossed into hot coals, hence the names given them by the English: "hoecakes" and "ashcakes." By observing the Indian cooks, the colonists soon learned to make the Indian breads the Indian way, to "bruse or pound them (the kernels) in a morter, and thereof make loaves or lumps of dowishe bread." "Dowishe" scarcely describes *corn pone,* however, for properly cooked, as they are in the South today, the cakes are light and crisp.

CORN PONE

(Makes 4 Pones)

> *1 cup corn meal*
> *½ teaspoon salt*
> *1 teaspoon baking powder*
> *2 tablespoons bacon drippings*
> *½ cup milk*

1. Mix corn meal, salt, and baking powder. Stir in bacon drippings and milk.
2. Grease a large, heavy skillet with bacon drippings. Drop batter from a tablespoon, shaping into 4 pones. Brown on both sides. Serve hot with lots of butter.

GOLDEN CORN BREAD

(Makes 8–10 Servings)

> 2 cups milk
> 1 teaspoon salt
> 1½ cups yellow corn meal
> ¾ cup butter or margarine
> 3 eggs, separated

1. Heat milk until just scalding. Stir in salt.
2. Quickly mix in the corn meal, beating until smooth. Add butter or margarine, and blend in well.
3. Beat egg yolks with a fork, and stir into the corn-meal mixture. Beat whites just until soft peaks will form; gently fold into the batter.
4. Bake the bread in a greased 8″ × 8″ × 2″ baking dish for 45 minutes in a moderate oven, 350°F.
5. Serve hot. Cut into squares, top with butter and wild honey or maple syrup.

Desserts

Southern Indian women, being both creative and experimental cooks, sweetened their corn-meal batter, mixed it with wild blackberries or strawberries, and baked the two together into a kind of *cobbler.*

BERRY CORN COBBLER

(Makes 6 Servings)

> 1 quart fresh strawberries or blackberries, washed (if you use strawberries, slice them in half)
> ½ cup sugar

1 cup corn meal
¼ cup sugar
1 teaspoon baking powder
1 teaspoon salt
½ cup sour milk
2 tablespoons melted butter or margarine

¼ cup honey
1 tablespoon melted butter or margarine
1 tablespoon lemon juice

1. Place berries in a 2-quart baking dish, and sprinkle with sugar.

2. For the topping, mix together all dry ingredients, then quickly stir in the milk and melted butter or margarine.

3. Drop batter by the tablespoon on top of berries, forming a design of rounds.

4. Mix together sauce ingredients, and pour over batter and exposed berries.

5. Bake in a moderately hot oven, 375°F., for 1 hour. Serve at room temperature.

HONEY TAPIOCA PUDDING

(Makes 6 Servings)

½ cup tapioca
½ cup water
¼ cup corn meal
3½ cups milk
⅔ cup honey
¼ teaspoon ginger
¼ teaspoon nutmeg
¼ teaspoon cinnamon

¼ teaspoon salt
1 tablespoon butter
2 eggs, lightly beaten

1. Soak the tapioca in the water for 1 hour. Then mix in the corn meal.

2. Combine the milk and honey, and blend the spices and salt with the butter.

3. Place the tapioca and corn meal, milk and honey, seasonings and butter in the top of a double boiler, and cook, stirring, for about 45 minutes or until the tapioca is transparent and tender.

4. Blend a little of the hot mixture into the eggs, then stir the eggs into the tapioca.

5. Pour into a buttered 1½-quart baking dish, set in a pan of water, and bake in a slow oven, 300°F., for 1 hour. Cool to room temperature, then chill and serve.

The Spanish oranges that the eighteenth-century naturalist William Bartram found growing throughout Florida were small and sour. The Seminoles, he discovered, had learned to make a delicacy of them by slicing off the tops and marinating the flesh of the orange in honey.

ORANGES MARINATED IN HONEY

(Makes 6 Servings)

6 large oranges
12 teaspoons honey

1. Wash the oranges well; slice off the tops, cutting about a third of the way down the orange. Using a sharp knife, loosen each section.

2. Spoon 2 teaspoons honey over each orange, re-

place tops, and let stand at room temperature for 24 hours before serving.

HOT SPICED APRICOTS

(Makes 4–6 Servings)

1 (11 oz.) box dried apricots
1 lemon, sliced
1 stick cinnamon
3 whole allspice
6 tablespoons maple syrup
Water for cooking

1. Place all ingredients in a medium-sized saucepan. Add enough water to make a depth of about ½ inch in the pan.

2. Simmer, stirring occasionally, for 30 minutes. Add more water if needed.

3. Serve hot as a dessert or as a spread for Squaw Bread.*

Though Hawaii seems home to the *pineapple*, it isn't.
Pineapples are actually native to tropical and subtropical areas of the Americas. Indians were particularly fond of this prickly fruit whether they ate it raw or roasted.

ROAST PINEAPPLE

(Makes 6 Servings)

> 1 pineapple
> 2 tablespoons honey

1. Slice the pineapple in half and score the flesh with a sharp knife. Spoon 1 tablespoon honey over each half.
2. Roast in a hot oven, 400°F., for 20 minutes. Cut each half into 3 pieces and serve.

Beverages

YAUPON TEA

(Makes 6–8 Servings)

> ⅓ cup dried yaupon leaves
> 1 quart water

Place the yaupon leaves and water in a saucepan and boil for 15 minutes. Strain and serve.

MINT TEA

(Makes 2 Quarts)

10 large stalks fresh mint, washed
2 quarts water

1. Place mint and water in a large saucepan, and bring slowly to a boil.
2. Turn off heat, cover, and let steep for 5 minutes.
3. Strain and serve.

HONEY DRINK

(Makes about 1 Quart)

1 quart water
⅔ cup honey

Place water and honey in a large jar with a close-fitting lid, and shake well to blend ingredients. Chill thoroughly, and serve iced in small glasses.

SASSAFRAS TEA

(Makes 1½ Quarts)

4 sassafras roots, each about 2" long
1½ quarts water

1. Scrub the roots well with a stiff brush, rinse, and scrape away the bark.

2. Place roots and bark scrapings along with the water in a large saucepan. Bring slowly to a boil, reduce heat, and simmer together gently for 15 minutes.

3. Turn off heat, and let tea steep for 10 minutes.

4. Strain and serve.

THE WOODSMEN OF THE EAST

THE WOODSMEN OF THE EAST

The land, the streams, and the lakes of the Eastern Woodlands filled the larders of the Indians living there. The earth itself was their oven. Along the Atlantic beaches, women of the Narragansett and Penobscot tribes dug deep pits in the sand, lined them with hot stones, filled them with shellfish and seaweed, and invented the clambake. They baked dried beans in much the same way, sometimes leaving them buried in the ground for several days to bubble gently with maple sugar. After such long and slow cooking, the beans came from the oven nutty and rich and lightly glazed with fragrant sugar syrup. A particular delicacy to these coastal tribes, as it is with us today, was the giant lobster, which the women steamed and seasoned with the sweet oil of sunflower seeds. The Iroquois of New York's Finger Lakes roasted succulent ears of green corn in the husk or baked young milky kernels into puddings and cakes. They picked tart wild cherries and simmered them with maple sugar; and also made an applesauce all the richer for the skins having been included. They smoked eel and blended them into savory stews, stuffed wild ducks with apples and grapes and turned them slowly over crackling flames so that the skin was browned and crisp, the meat tender as butter.

As you can see, Indian women of the Eastern Woodlands were particularly accomplished and creative cooks. Also, as among the Hopi of Arizona and others, they occupied a place of respect within the family because it was through them that the lineage descended. The Iroquois women were property owners. The longhouses, or communal lodges, belonged to them as did the fields and the crops.

At corn-planting time, whole villages of women would go to the fields and offer a prayer, each repeating, "God, our Father, you see me and my children. We stand in the middle of the field where we are going to plant our food. We beg you to supply us with an abundant yield of corn." Sometimes the men of the families chanted prayers too: "In the sky you live, Haweni'yu'. We are ready to place in the ground the corn upon which we live. We ask for assistance and that we may have a plentiful crop."

Then the women began to work. Together they sowed the seed, weeded the rows, and gathered the bounty, not only because many hands made light of their labor, but also because they simply enjoyed one another's company. Fields rang with song as they tended their crops. "First hoeing . . . second hoeing . . . I am through hoeing . . . I am planting corn . . . the corn is sprouting . . . the ears are forming . . . the silk is forming . . . the pollen is being shed . . . the corn is in the milk . . . the green corn is ready for use . . . the corn is getting ripe."

Europeans first traveling among the various eastern tribes found them a hospitable people. Whenever a stranger entered a longhouse, the woman's first duty was to set food and tobacco before him. Neglecting to do so was considered an inexcusable affront. Only after the visitor had dined to his satisfaction was he asked to state the nature of his business.

Unlike the Salish, Tlingit, and others of the Northwest Coast, most eastern tribes enjoyed only one full meal a day—a combination of breakfast and lunch, which they ate before noon. This was the time for hearty food, a robust rack of game or broiled fish, a crisp salad, baked pumpkin or squash, crunchy hazelnut cakes. The men ate first, usually from wooden or earthenware bowls. Afterward, the women and children ate what was left. Meals were usually silent affairs with each family member sitting or standing. If a guest was present, it was etiquette for him to say, upon finishing his meal, "Thanks," to which his host would reply, "It is well." Parents carefully disciplined their children and taught them to give thanks for each meal. If a child failed to do so, he was told he would be punished by a stomach ache. Though there was no formal breakfast or supper, there was always food on hand, usually a gruel or hominy, for those who were hungry in the morning and evening, and for the stranger who might wander into the village.

John Bartram visited the Iroquois in 1743 and described a feast he was served: "This repast consisted of three great kettles of Indian corn soup, or thin hominy, with dry'd eels and other fish boiled in it, and one kettle full of young squashes and their flowers boiled in water, and a little meal mixed . . . last of all was served a great bowl full of Indian dumplings, made of new soft corn, cut or scraped off the ear, then with the addition of some boiled beans, lapped well up in Indian corn leaves, this is good hearty provision."

Feasts and ceremonies were popular among the Eastern Woodlands tribes, particularly among the Cayuga, Seneca, Oneida, Onandaga, and Mohawk, who comprised the Iroquois League. Most were solemn, religious affairs, seasonal thanksgivings: the Maple, Planting, Strawberry, Green Corn, Harvest, and New Year's festivals.

The woodsmen of the East could be thankful for a land that was good to them. As you will see in the following recipes, we today can be thankful to these tribes for many dishes that have become New England classics, including soufflé-light codfish balls, clam chowder, Boston brown bread, cranberry pudding as moist and feathery as the finest of England, satin-smooth pumpkin soups, wild beach plum jam. Indeed, we have the Indian to thank for the very idea of Thanksgiving.

Soups

SUNFLOWER SEED SOUP

(Makes 6 Servings)

2 cups shelled sunflower seeds
3 scallions, washed and sliced (include tops)
6 cups water
2 (5.4 gram) packages instant chicken broth
1 teaspoon salt

Place all ingredients in a large saucepan and simmer, stirring occasionally, for 45 minutes. Serve hot.

The Iroquois were blessed with clear, cool lakes and sparkling streams, and both served up an abundance of *fish*. Fish soup, or *u'nega'gei'*, as the Iroquois called it, was a favorite. One early recipe is described, "Fish of any kind is boiled in a pot with a quantity of water. It is then removed and coarse corn siftings stirred in to make a soup of suitable consistency." When wild onions and greens were available, they were usually tossed into the soup pot, adding both color and flavor.

IROQUOIS SOUP

(Makes 4–6 Servings)

4 large mushrooms, wiped and sliced
2 (10½ oz.) cans beef consommé
2 tablespoons yellow corn meal
2 tablespoons minced parsley
1 clove garlic, peeled and crushed
½ teaspoon basil
1 medium yellow onion, peeled and thinly sliced
Dash fresh ground pepper
¼ teaspoon salt
1 (12 oz.) package frozen haddock fillets
1 (10 oz.) package frozen baby Lima beans
⅓ cup dry sherry (optional)

1. Place the mushrooms, consommé, corn meal, parsley, garlic, basil, onion, pepper, and salt in a large saucepan, and simmer, uncovered, for 10 minutes.

2. Add haddock, Lima beans, and if you like, sherry, and simmer 20 minutes, stirring occasionally and breaking the haddock into bite-sized pieces. Serve hot.

SCALLOP SOUP

(Makes 6 Servings)

>   2 pounds fresh scallops
>   6 cups water
>   2 scallions, washed and sliced (include tops)
>   ½ cup washed water cress sprigs
>   1½ teaspoons salt
>   ⅛ teaspoon fresh ground pepper

Place scallops, water, scallions, and water cress in a large saucepan, and simmer gently for 30 minutes. Season with salt and pepper, and serve.

PEA BEAN AND POTATO SOUP

(Makes 10–12 Servings)

>   ⅔ pound pea beans
>   4 medium potatoes, peeled
>   3 tablespoons butter
>   4 teaspoons salt
>   ½ teaspoon fresh ground pepper
>   ⅓ cup minced scallions or chives

1. Wash, soak, and cook the pea beans according to package directions. Reserve the cooking water.
2. Cover the potatoes with water and boil until tender. Drain, saving the cooking water.
3. Measure the bean-cooking water and add enough of the potato water to make 6 cups of liquid. Pour into a large saucepan. Mash the beans and the potatoes, and add to the saucepan along with the remaining ingredients.
4. Simmer together very slowly for 1 hour. Serve

hot or cold. When serving cold, thin, if you like, with water.

Pumpkins, the "pompions" of early English diaries, were prepared in every conceivable manner. They were baked whole in hot ashes, cooked in broth as a vegetable, mashed and served with butter like potatoes, and, as an Oneida recipe instructs, "boiled with meat to the consistency of potato soup."

PUMPKIN SOUP

(Makes 10–12 Servings)

1 (1 lb. 13 oz.) can water-pack pumpkin purée
1 quart milk
2 tablespoons butter or margarine
2 tablespoons honey
2 tablespoons maple sugar or light brown sugar
½ teaspoon powdered marjoram
Dash fresh ground pepper
¼ teaspoon cinnamon
¼ teaspoon mace
1 teaspoon salt
Juice of 1 orange

1. Heat pumpkin purée, milk, butter, and honey together slowly in a large saucepan, stirring.

2. Combine maple sugar, marjoram, pepper, cinnamon, mace, and salt, and stir into pumpkin-milk mixture. Heat slowly, stirring, to simmering point. Do not boil.

3. Add the orange juice, a little at a time, stirring constantly. Serve hot. Or for a refreshing summer soup, thin mixture with 2 cups milk, chill, and serve icy cold.

Squash was almost as important as corn to the Iroquois and other woodsmen of the East because of its nourishment and versatility. Women frequently baked squash whole, particularly the rich, sweet-meated acorn and butternut varieties, using fat and honey or maple syrup for seasoning. The delicate yellow summer squashes were sometimes boiled and blended into a smooth, fragrant soup. Like corn, squash was also of ceremonial importance. The rattles used by the Medicine Societies were sometimes made from the long-handled calabash or gourd, although summer crookneck squash was also used.

YELLOW SQUASH SOUP

(Makes 6–8 Servings)

2 pounds yellow squash, washed and sliced
2 scallions, washed and sliced (include tops)
1 quart water
1 tablespoon honey
1 tablespoon fresh minced dill
1 tablespoon salt
⅛ teaspoon fresh ground pepper

1. Place the squash, scallions, water, and honey in a large saucepan, and simmer gently for about 40 minutes or until squash is tender. Stir in the dill.

2. Put the squash through a food mill or purée in a blender until smooth.

3. Return to saucepan, season with salt and pepper, and simmer for 5 to 10 minutes more. Serve hot or chill and serve cold. If you serve the soup cold, you may have to thin it a little with water.

FRESH TOMATO SOUP

(Makes 8–10 Servings)

4 pounds tomatoes, washed and halved
1 greening or other cooking apple, peeled, cored and quartered
2 yellow onions, peeled and sliced
2 sprigs mint
6 sprigs fresh dill
2 (5.4 gram) packages instant chicken broth
2 bay leaves
1 teaspoon salt
2 quarts water

Place all ingredients in a large, heavy kettle, and simmer very slowly, stirring occasionally, for 3 hours. Remove bay leaves and serve hot or chilled.

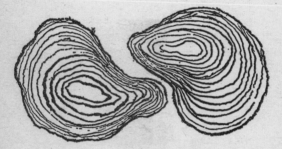

OYSTER SOUP

(Makes 6 Servings)

> 2 dozen shucked oysters and their juice
> ¼ cup butter
> 2 cups milk
> ¼ cup corn meal
> ½ teaspoon salt
> ⅛ teaspoon fresh ground pepper

1. Place the oysters, oyster juice, and butter in a large saucepan.

2. Mix ¼ cup milk with the corn meal, then stir into the rest of the milk, and add to the oysters.

3. Heat very gently, stirring, for about 25 minutes. Season with salt and pepper, and serve.

Nut meats and certain sweet acorns were not only eaten raw by the Algonquin people but also pounded into a meal and used in breads and soups. The breads actually were cakes made by mixing the nut meal with corn meal and frying in hot fat. Nut oils were extracted by boiling and used as seasoning for vegetables and as spreads for bread. Thomas Hariot, the English colonist, described a method common among the Powhatan of Virginia that was similar to that of the Algonquin: "besides their eating of them after our ordinary manner, they break them with stones and pound them in morters with water to make a milk which they use to put into some sorts of their spoone-meat; also among their sodden wheat, peaze, beanes and pompions which maketh them have a farre more pleasant taste."

HAZELNUT SOUP

(Makes 4–6 Servings)

> *2¼ cups ground, unblanched hazelnuts*
> *2 (4.5 gram) packages instant beef broth*
> *2 scallions, washed and sliced*
> *2 tablespoons minced parsley*
> *5 cups water*
> *1 teaspoon salt*
> *⅛ teaspoon fresh ground pepper*

Place all ingredients in a large saucepan, and simmer together gently, stirring occasionally, for 1 hour. Serve hot. Make the servings small; the soup is rich.

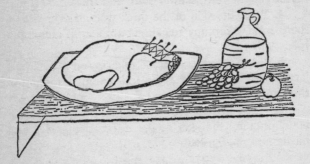

ROAST DUCK STUFFED WITH APPLES AND GRAPES

(Makes 4–6 Servings)

1 (5½ lb.) duck, dressed

STUFFING:

Duck giblets
½ pound mushrooms, wiped and coarsely chopped
4 greening apples, cored and sliced (do not peel)
1½ cups washed, halved, and seeded Tokay or other
*   sweet grapes*
2 cups unblanched hazelnuts
1 teaspoon salt

FOR BASTING:

2 cups apple cider

1. Cover the duck giblets with water in a small saucepan, and simmer gently for ½ hour. Drain, reserving ½ cup of the giblet-cooking water. Chop the giblets for the stuffing.

2. Mix the giblets and ½ cup giblet-cooking water with the stuffing ingredients.

3. Remove any pinfeathers from the duck, and singe to remove any hairs. Stuff both neck and body cavities of the bird, skewer shut, and truss.

4. Prick the skin of the duck well all over with a sharp fork. Wrap any remaining stuffing in aluminum foil.

5. Place the duck, breast side up, on a rack in a large roasting pan. Place the foil-wrapped stuffing in the pan beside the bird.

6. Place in a hot oven, 400°F., and roast for 1 hour, pricking the skin of the duck with a fork and basting every 20 minutes with cider.

7. Reduce oven temperature to moderate, 350°F., and continue to roast for 2 hours more, pricking the duck and basting every 20 minutes with cider and drippings.

ROAST GOOSE

(Makes 8–10 Servings)

1 (10–11 lb.) goose

STUFFING:

Goose giblets
1 quart water
2 (8 oz.) packages prepared poultry stuffing
2 cups fresh cranberries, washed and mashed
¼ pound fresh mushrooms, wiped and chopped
1 (1 lb.) can sweetened plums, pitted (reserve syrup)
1 tablespoon salt
¼ teaspoon fresh ground pepper

BASTING:

2 cups apple cider

1. Simmer the goose giblets in 1 quart water for about 30 minutes or until tender. Chop the giblets. Skim the cooking water of fat, and save.

2. For the stuffing, mix together the prepared poultry stuffing, mashed cranberries, mushrooms, plums and their syrup, salt, pepper, giblets and their cooking broth.

3. Remove any pinfeathers from the goose, and singe off hairs. Stuff neck and body cavities, skewer shut, and truss.

4. Place breast side up on a rack in a large roasting pan and roast, uncovered, in a moderate oven, 350°F., for 4½ hours. Prick the skin of the goose well from time to time and baste every 15 minutes with the cider and drippings.

Eels and fish were favorite foods among the Eastern Woodlands tribes. Both were taken from the rivers fresh and broiled or dried and smoked for winter eating. The French Jesuits who traveled down the St. Lawrence and into Finger Lake country often mentioned eels in their accounts and the Indian way of broiling them on sapling sticks or boiling them into a thick soup.

SMOKED EEL STEW

(Makes 6–8 Servings)

1 (1½ lb.) smoked eel, cut into 2" pieces
4 potatoes, washed but not peeled
4 yellow onions, peeled
6 cups water
⅛ teaspoon fresh ground pepper

Simmer all together in a large heavy kettle for about 1 hour or until the potatoes are tender. Skim off excess fat. Serve hot.

STEAMED MUSSELS AND HALIBUT

(Makes 4 Servings)

2 dozen mussels
2 center slices of halibut weighing about 1 pound
   each
¼ cup butter or margarine
2 scallions, washed and sliced (include tops)
¼ cup minced parsley
½ teaspoon dill seed
Pinch fresh ground pepper
Salt to season

1. Scrub mussels well with a stiff brush.
2. Place a large strip of heavy-duty aluminum foil (about 2' long) in a shallow baking pan so that the sides hang over the edge.
3. Lay the two pieces of halibut on the foil in the pan, dot with butter or margarine, top with sliced scallions, minced parsley, dill seed, and fresh ground pepper.

4. Place mussels around the fish. Wrap all in aluminum foil, pressing the edges together to make a tight package which will seal in the steam and juices.

5. Bake for 45 minutes in a moderate oven, 350° F. Unwrap, sprinkle lightly with salt, and serve.

Although a Frenchman sailing off Cape Cod is credited with inventing *clam chowder*, the Eastern Woodlands Indians were making a simple version years earlier. According to one recipe, "The bivalves are boiled and made into soup. Milk, salt and butter are frequently added." Most popular of the shellfish were mussels, oysters, and clams, which were "made use of by the Indians who eat them after five or six hours boiling to make them tender."

CLAM CHOWDER

(Makes 6 Servings)

> 3 slices bacon, cut into julienne strips
> 2 yellow onions, peeled and minced
> 2 dozen fresh clams out of the shell
> 2 tablespoons butter or margarine
> 2 tablespoons flour
> 2 cups water
> 6 new potatoes, peeled and diced
> 1 teaspoon salt
> ⅛ teaspoon fresh ground pepper

1. Brown the bacon in a large saucepan, add the onions, and sauté until golden.

2. Chop the clams, drain, and save liquid. Add the clams to the kettle, then mix in the butter or margarine and flour. Heat, stirring, for about 2 minutes.

3. Stir in the clam juice and water, then add the potatoes, salt, and pepper. Simmer, covered, for 2 hours, stirring occasionally. Serve hot.

STEAMED HEN AND VEGETABLES

(Makes 8 Servings)

1 (4½ lb.) hen
2 quarts water
2 tablespoons salt
14 new potatoes, washed
8 mushrooms, wiped
6 yellow onions, peeled
½ pound fresh green beans, washed and snapped
¼ teaspoon fresh ground pepper

1. Place the hen and the giblets in a large, heavy kettle. Add the water; cover, and simmer for 45 minutes.

2. Stir in the salt, arrange the vegetables in and around the hen, season all with pepper, cover, and simmer for 1 hour longer.

3. Slice off pieces of chicken, and serve hot with vegetables and broth in a soup bowl.

CODFISH BALLS

(Makes 8–10 Servings)

2¾ pounds fresh cod
1 quart raw diced potatoes
2 cups water
2 tablespoons butter
2 teaspoons salt
¼ teaspoon fresh ground pepper
1 quart fat or oil for deep-fat frying

1. Place the cod, potatoes, and water in a large saucepan and boil, covered, for 25 minutes. Drain well and mash.

2. Season the mixture with butter, salt, and pepper. Roll into 2″ balls.

3. Heat the fat or oil in a large heavy kettle until it registers 375° F. on a deep-fat-frying thermometer. Drop the codfish balls in, and fry, stirring, until golden brown on all sides.

The English and Dutch settling in the territories of the Eastern Woodlands Indian had never seen *shellfish* of such awesome dimension as the lobster, or any fish of sweeter flesh. The Dutch pulled lobsters six feet long from the waters of New Amsterdam, but Adriaen Van der Donck noted: "Those a foot long are better for serving at the table." The European way of preparing lobster was the Indian way—they were steamed, boiled in seawater, or layered with clams and other shellfish in a clambake.

CLAMBAKE

(Makes 6–8 Servings)

> 2 dozen oysters in the shell
> 3 dozen mussels in the shell
> 2 dozen clams in the shell
> 6 ears of corn in the husk
> 6 medium-sized potatoes, unpeeled
> 6 (1¼–1½ lb.) green lobsters
> 2 quarts water mixed with 2 tablespoons salt

1. Scrub the oysters, mussels, and clams well with a stiff brush. Rinse well in cold water.

2. Peel the outer layers of husk from each ear of corn.

3. Scrub the potatoes well.

4. For the clambake, you will need a large, heavy kettle with a tight-fitting lid. Place the oysters in the bottom of the kettle. Add 3 lobsters, 3 ears of corn, the 6 potatoes, the remaining 3 ears of corn, and 3 lobsters, arranging each ingredient as nearly as possible in layers.

5. Add the mussels and clams, dropping them in and around the other foods.

6. Pour the salt water over all, cover, and bring to a boil. Reduce heat, and simmer for 2 hours or until potatoes are done. Serve at once.

BAKED STUFFED SEA BASS

(Makes 6 Servings)

> 1 (3–4 lb.) sea bass or halibut, split and cleaned
> 1 cup finely chopped mushrooms
> 2 tablespoons cooking oil
> 1 cup chopped chestnuts
> 1 scallion, washed and chopped (include tops)
> 1 clove garlic, peeled and crushed
> 2 cups prepared poultry stuffing
> 1 (10 oz.) can of frozen shrimp or oyster soup, thawed
> 1 teaspoon salt
> 1/8 teaspoon fresh ground pepper
> 3/4 cup apple cider

1. Wipe the fish lightly inside and out with a damp cloth and sprinkle with salt.

189

2. Sauté the mushrooms in the oil until golden brown. Drain on paper toweling.

3. Mix together the mushrooms, nuts, scallion, garlic, prepared poultry stuffing, thawed soup, salt, and pepper, and stuff the fish with the mixture. Lay the fish on a large piece of heavy-duty aluminum foil, and wrap, leaving a small vent at the top for basting.

4. Place the wrapped fish in a baking pan and bake in a moderate oven, 350° F., for 1 hour, basting from time to time with the apple cider.

Vegetables

BOSTON BAKED BEANS

(Makes 6 Servings)

> *1 pound dried navy beans*
> *Water for cooking*
> *½ pound salt pork, cut into 4 pieces*
> *½ cup molasses*
> *1 teaspoon salt*
> *1 teaspoon dry mustard*
> *4 tablespoons maple sugar*
> *½ teaspoon baking soda*
> *1 onion, peeled and sliced*
> *¼ cup brandy (optional)*

1. Place the beans in a large saucepan; add enough water to come about 2″ above the surface of the beans.

2. Add the salt pork, and simmer the beans very slowly for about 2 hours or until just tender. Add more water as needed from time to time.

3. Drain the beans, reserving ½ cup of the cooking water.

4. In a measuring cup, combine molasses, salt, dry mustard, and maple sugar. Add enough of the bean cooking water to measure 1 cup. Mix in soda.

5. Stir mixture into the beans along with the sliced onions and, if you like, the brandy.

6. Transfer beans to a 2-quart bean pot and bake for 1½ to 2 hours in a moderately slow oven, 325° F. There should be just enough liquid in the beans to bubble up. Serve at once.

BAKED PUMPKIN

(Makes 6–8 Servings)

1 small pumpkin
2 tablespoons honey
2 tablespoons apple cider
2 tablespoons melted butter or margarine

1. Wash the pumpkin well, place on a pie tin, and bake in a moderate oven, 350° F., for 1½ hours.

2. Remove from the oven and cut a hole in the top of the pumpkin about 3 to 4 inches in diameter. Scoop out pulp and seeds.

3. Mix together the honey, cider, and melted butter or margarine. Baste the mixture over the flesh of the pumpkin. Replace top, return to a moderate oven

and continue to bake for 35 to 40 minutes longer, basting occasionally.

4. Serve whole, scooping out the individual portions at the table. Or cut into wedges as you would a melon. Ladle a little of the cider mixture over each serving.

BOILED CORN PUDDING

(Makes 8–10 Servings)

> 2 (10 oz.) packages frozen whole kernel corn
> 2 quarts chicken broth
> ¼ cup butter or margarine
> 1⅓ cups white corn meal
> ½ cup flour
> 2 teaspoons baking powder
> 1 tablespoon sugar
> 1 teaspoon salt
> 1 egg
> Milk

1. Place the frozen corn in a strainer to thaw. Reserve liquid.

2. Heat the chicken broth and butter in a large kettle and let simmer for 5 minutes.

3. Sift together the corn meal, flour, baking powder, sugar, and salt. Measure the liquid from the thawed corn, add enough milk to bring the measure to ½ cup, then beat this mixture with the egg until light. Quickly mix the liquid ingredients into the dry, and fold in the corn.

4. Bring the chicken broth to a rapid boil, then drop in the corn batter a tablespoonful at a time.

5. Reduce heat, cover, and simmer for 15 minutes. Uncover, stir well, and serve as a potato substitute.

BOILED BUTTERNUT SQUASH

(Makes 4 Servings)

1 large butternut squash, washed
2 cups chicken or beef stock
3 scallions, washed and sliced
2 tablespoons butter or chicken fat
½ teaspoon salt
⅛ teaspoon fresh ground pepper

1. Cut the squash in half and remove pulp and seeds. Slice into large chunks.

2. Place squash and remaining ingredients in a large saucepan and simmer, covered, for about 30 minutes or until tender. Serve in bowls, topped with some of the broth.

BAKED BUTTERNUT SQUASH

(Makes 6–8 Servings)

2 butternut squashes, washed
4 tablespoons butter
4 tablespoons honey
4 teaspoons maple sugar
Salt
Pepper
Nutmeg

1. Place the whole squashes on a baking sheet and bake in a moderately slow oven, 325° F., for about 1 hour or until a fork will pierce them.

2. Remove from the oven, cut in half, scoop out pulp and seeds. Dot each half with 1 tablespoon but-

ter and 1 tablespoon honey; sprinkle each with 1 teaspoon maple sugar, then season each lightly with salt, pepper, and nutmeg.

3. Return to the oven and continue to bake in a moderately slow oven, 325° F., for about 1 hour and 20 minutes longer or until the flesh is tender. Baste occasionally with the honey-butter mixture that has collected in the hollow of each squash.

4. To serve, cut the pieces of squash in half and spoon some of the honey-butter drippings over each.

STEWED TOMATOES

(Makes 6 Servings)

> 3 pounds tomatoes, washed and cored
> 12 scallions, washed and the tops removed
> ¼ cup water
> ¼ cup minced fresh dill
> 1 teaspoon salt
> ⅛ teaspoon fresh ground pepper
> ¼ cup corn meal

1. Place the tomatoes, cored side down, in a large saucepan. Add the scallions and water and simmer very slowly, stirring occasionally, for about 30 minutes.

2. Stir in the dill, salt, and pepper, and simmer about 10 minutes more or until tomatoes are tender and slightly broken up.

3. Quickly stir in the corn meal, adding it a tablespoon at a time. Simmer for about 5 minutes longer and serve.

Though *leeks* are usually associated with France, a fragrant wild variety did grow in the Eastern Woodlands of the United States. Indian women used both tops and stems for preparing soups, salads, and vegetable dishes, and for seasoning meat stews.

LEEKS AND NEW POTATOES

(Makes 4–6 Servings)

> 10 new potatoes, washed
> 3 large leeks, washed and quartered
> 1 (1½") cube fat back
> 2 cups water
> 1 teaspoon salt
> ⅛ teaspoon fresh ground pepper

1. Place all ingredients in a large saucepan, and boil, uncovered, for 25 minutes or until the potatoes are tender.
2. Serve in bowls, spooning broth over each portion.

SALAD OF WILD GREENS

(Makes 4 Servings)

SALAD:

¾ cup sliced scallion tops, washed
1 quart tender young water cress sprigs, washed
1½ cups field salad, washed

DRESSING:

⅓ cup salad oil
¼ cup cider vinegar
2 tablespoons honey
1 teaspoon salt
⅛ teaspoon fresh ground pepper

1. Place the salad greens in a large wooden bowl, and toss lightly to mix.

2. Combine the dressing ingredients in a shaker jar, and shake well to blend.

3. Dress the salad, toss again, and serve.

GRUEL

(Makes 6–8 Servings)

> 3½ cups water
> 1¼ cups white corn meal
> 1½ teaspoons salt
> Butter

1. Bring the water to a boil. Mix together the corn meal and salt.
2. Pour the boiling water over the meal, stirring. Heat the gruel slowly, stirring, for 5 minutes or until smooth and thick.
3. Serve in bowls. Top with lumps of butter.

FRIED GRUEL

(Makes 6–8 Servings)

> 1 recipe Gruel
> ¼ cup bacon drippings

1. When the gruel is room temperature, pack it into two (10 oz.) drinking glasses. Chill several hours until firm.
2. Unmold the gruel, slice into rounds about ½ inch thick, and brown well on both sides in the bacon drippings. Serve hot as a bread or topped with melted butter and honey or maple syrup as a breakfast dish.

HAZELNUT CAKES

(Makes 12–14 Small Cakes)

> ½ pound unblanched hazelnuts, ground or puréed in
> a blender
> 2 cups water
> ⅓ cup corn meal
> 1 teaspoon salt
> ½ cup cooking oil

1. Boil the ground nuts in the water, stirring occasionally, for 30 minutes or until the mixture is the consistency of a mush.

2. Mix in the corn meal and salt and let stand for about 20 minutes or until thick.

3. Heat the oil in a large heavy skillet until a drop of water sizzles. Drop the nut mixture from a tablespoon. Brown well on one side, turn, flatten into a cake with a well-greased spatula, and brown. Serve hot or cold as a bread.

SUNFLOWER SEED CAKES

(Makes about 15 Cakes)

> 3 cups shelled sunflower seeds
> 3 cups water
> 2¼ teaspoons salt
> 6 tablespoons white corn meal
> ½ cup cooking oil or shortening

1. Place sunflower seeds, water, and salt in a large saucepan, cover, and simmer for 1 hour, stirring occasionally. Put the mixture through a food mill or purée in a blender.

2. Mix in the corn meal, a tablespoon at a time, to make a dough stiff enough to be shaped with the hands. Cool to room temperature.

3. Shape into firm, flat cakes about 3 inches in diameter.

4. Heat the oil in a large, heavy skillet until a drop of water sizzles. Brown the cakes well on both sides, and drain on paper toweling. Add more oil as needed when browning the cakes.

INDIAN BREAD

(Makes 10–12 Servings)

3 cups flour
1¾ cups corn meal
1 teaspoon soda
2 teaspoons salt
¼ teaspoon nutmeg
3⅓ cups milk
1 cup molasses

1. Sift together the dry ingredients. Combine the milk and molasses.

2. Add the liquid ingredients to the dry ingredients, and beat with a rotary beater until smooth.

3. Pour into a well-greased 2-quart steam mold, cover, and place on a rack in a deep kettle that has a close-fitting lid.

4. Pour enough boiling water into the kettle to come about half way up the mold. Cover the kettle and steam the mold for 3 hours.

5. Remove the mold from the kettle, and let stand 20 minutes. Remove the cover, and let stand 10 minutes longer. Loosen the edges of the pudding with a spatula, invert the mold on a plate, and let stand until the pudding unmolds.

6. Serve with lots of butter.

Desserts

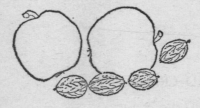

APPLES ROASTED OVER HOT COALS

(Makes 6 Servings)

6 greenings or other baking apples

1. Wash the apples well, remove stems, and wrap in heavy aluminum foil.

2. Place over glowing coals. Charcoal briquettes, prepared for broiling meat, work well.

3. Roast for 8 minutes; turn the apples and roast for 8 minutes more. Serve hot.

APPLESAUCE

(Makes 6–8 Servings)

  3 pounds greenings
  1 (6 oz.) package maple sugar
  3 cups water

1. Wash apples thoroughly, core but do not peel, and cut into wedges.

2. Place apples, maple sugar, and water in a large saucepan, bring slowly to a boil, then reduce heat and simmer, stirring occasionally, for 40 minutes. Serve hot or cold.

STEAMED CRANBERRY PUDDING

  ¼ cup butter or margarine
  ½ cup sugar
  1 cup honey
  4 eggs, beaten until light
  1 cup chopped fresh cranberries
  3 cups flour
  3 teaspoons baking powder
  1 teaspoon salt

1. Cream butter or margarine with sugar and honey until smooth.

2. Fold in the beaten eggs along with the chopped cranberries.

3. Sift flour with baking powder and salt, and mix in, a little at a time.

4. Pour batter into a 1½-quart greased and floured pudding mold which has a tight-fitting cover.

5. Place a rack in a large pot, stand sealed mold on the rack, and add enough boiling water to half cover the mold. Regulate burner so that the water will continue to boil gently.

6. Cover the pot and steam the mold for 2 hours.

7. Cool slightly, unmold pudding onto a dessert platter, and serve.

INDIAN PUDDING

(Makes 6–8 Servings)

> 1½ cups seedless raisins
> 3 cups scalded milk
> 1½ cups cold milk
> 1 cup corn meal
> ½ cup molasses
> 1 teaspoon salt
> ½ cup sugar
> ¾ teaspoon ginger
> ¼ teaspoon nutmeg
> ¼ cup butter

1. Add the raisins to the hot milk. Mix 1 cup cold milk with the corn meal, then stir into the hot milk. Heat very slowly, stirring constantly, for about 10 to 15 minutes or until the mixture thickens.

2. Mix in the molasses, salt, sugar, ginger, nutmeg, and butter. Pour into a buttered 2-quart casserole. Then pour the remaining ½ cup cold milk into the center of the pudding.

3. Set dish in a pan of cold water, and bake in a slow oven, 300° F., for 2½ hours. Let cool for 3 to 4 hours before serving.

GOOSEBERRY COBBLER

(Makes 6 Servings)

>2 cups flour
>½ cup corn meal plus 2 tablespoons
>½ teaspoon baking powder
>1 teaspoon salt
>¾ cup butter or margarine
>¾ cup boiling water
>2 (15 oz.) cans sweetened whole gooseberries
>1 teaspoon honey
>Juice of ½ lemon

1. Sift the flour with ½ cup corn meal, the baking powder, and salt. Using a pastry blender or two knives, cut in the butter or margarine. Quickly add the boiling water, mixing in well.

2. Divide the dough in half, and pat half of it in a buttered 8″ × 8″ × 2″ baking pan. Sprinkle with 1 tablespoon corn meal.

3. Mash half of the gooseberries in their syrup, then stir in remaining gooseberries, honey, and lemon juice. Pour over the dough.

4. Top with remaining dough; sprinkle with remaining tablespoon corn meal.

5. Bake in a very hot oven, 425° F., for 30 minutes or until top is lightly browned. Cut into squares and serve.

Almost all early accounts of explorers in the Eastern Woodlands mention *maple syrup.* In 1671 the Jesuit Nouvel referred to a "liquor that runs from the trees toward the end of Winter, and which is known as Maple-water." Although the Indians did tap maple trees and collect the sap, their primitive utensils kept them from boiling it into sugar. With the arrival of

Europeans and iron pots, however, the Indians quickly learned to do so. Their sugar molds were "broad, wooden dishes of about two inches in depth." The crystallizing syrup was "stirred about in these until cold." Maple syrups and sugars were highly prized and used to sweeten cooked fruits and to mellow the flavor of dried corn soups.

CHERRIES SIMMERED WITH MAPLE SUGAR

(Makes 4–6 Servings)

2 (1 lb.) cans water-pack tart red pitted cherries
1 cup maple sugar

1. Place the cherry juice and maple sugar in a saucepan and boil for 10 minutes.
2. Drop in the cherries and simmer for 5 minutes. Serve hot or cold.

CRANBERRY SAUCE

(Makes about 1 Quart)

1 pound fresh cranberries, washed
1 cup maple sugar
1 cup sugar
1¼ cups water

1. Place all ingredients in a large saucepan, bring to a boil, reduce heat, and simmer for about 20 minutes or until the cranberry skins pop.

2. Cool to room temperature or chill and serve.

Confections

MAPLE-SUGARED NUTS AND FRUITS

(Makes 10–12 Servings)

1 cup maple sugar
½ cup water
½ cup unblanched walnut halves
½ cup unblanched filberts
1½ cups dried prunes or apricots

1. Place maple sugar and water in a small, deep saucepan and heat slowly, without stirring, to the soft-ball stage, 238° F. on a candy thermometer.

2. Remove from the heat, drop the walnuts into the hot syrup, turn gently with a spoon so that they are evenly coated. Remove to aluminum foil with a slotted spoon. Repeat with the filberts.

3. Dip the prunes or apricots into the hot syrup with tongs, making sure that they are evenly coated. If the syrup begins to harden, heat just long enough to melt it. Remove prunes to a strip of aluminum foil.

4. Cool the nuts and fruit to room temperature. Then serve as a confection.

BEACH PLUM JAM

(Makes about 8 (6 oz.) Jars)

2 quarts beach plums, washed and picked over
1 cup water
8 cups sugar
Melted paraffin

1. Place the beach plums and water in a large saucepan and cook over a low heat for about 15 minutes or until the fruit is soft.

2. Remove from the heat and cool. Seed the plums, taking care not to mash them.

3. Return the fruit and juice to the saucepan, add the sugar, and mix well. Boil, stirring constantly, for 15 minutes.

4. Skim froth from the jam, spoon mixture into jam jars, and seal with paraffin.

MAPLE DRINK

(Makes 6–8 Servings)

    ½ cup maple sugar
    6 cups water

1. Place together in a large saucepan and simmer, stirring occasionally, for 15 minutes.
2. Serve hot or chill and serve over ice.

APPENDIX

APPETIZERS

Avocado and Piñon Nut Appetizer

Batter-fried Squash Blossoms

Western Chili Dip

Guacamole

Jerusalem Artichokes as an Appetizer

Fresh Roasted Peanuts

Fresh Roasted Piñon Nuts

Octopus Fritters

Smoked Salmon or Red Caviar Spread for Buckskin Bread

SOUPS

Beef Balls in Saffron Broth

Black Bean Soup

Lima Bean and Tomato Soup

Pea Bean and Potato Soup

Pinto Bean Spoon Soup

Corn Chowder

Corn and Dried Beef Soup

Dried Corn Soup

Fish and Spinach Broth

Hazelnut Soup

Hominy Soup

Iroquois Soup

Jerusalem Artichoke Soup

Mushroom Soup

Nut and Mint Soup

Peanut Soup

Piñon Soup

Peppery Potato-Tomato Soup

Pumpkin Soup

Oyster Soup

Scallion Soup

Scallop Soup

Smoked Salmon Soup

Yellow Squash Soup

Sunflower Seed Soup

Fresh Tomato Soup

Trout Consommé

Turtle Soup

Water Cress Soup

GAME

Charcoal-broiled Buffalo Steaks

Roast Duck Stuffed with Apples and Grapes

Stewed Wild Rabbit with Dumplings

Broiled Reindeerburgers

Broiled Venison Steak

Game Hens with Wild Rice-Hazelnut Stuffing

Roast Goose

Roast Pheasant Stuffed with Grapes and Nuts

Green Peppers Stuffed with Venison

Roast Saddle of Venison

Venison and Wild Rice Stew

MEATS

Barbecued Pork Roast

Sautéed Brains

Chili Rio Grande

Lamb Stew with Squaw Bread Dumplings

Lamb-Stuffed Sweet Red Peppers

Pueblo Lamb Shanks

Tamales

Peppery Tripe Stew

Zuñi Green Chili Stew

POULTRY AND EGGS

Brunswick Stew

Chicken Baked with Scallions, Mushrooms, and Tomatoes

Chippewa Wild Rice

Eggs Scrambled with Smoked Salmon

Eggs and Wild Onions

Steamed Hen and Vegetables

Turkey with Oyster-Cornbread Stuffing

SEAFOOD

Baked Stuffed Sea Bass

Clambake

Clam Chowder

Codfish Balls

Boiled Blue Crabs

Broiled Alaskan King Crab

Smoked Eel Stew

Flounder with Mussel Sauce

Batter-fried Frogs Legs

Halibut Aspic

Steamed Mussels with Butter Sauce

Steamed Mussels and Halibut

Pompano Steamed with Grapes

Red Snapper Baked with Oranges

SEAFOOD

Salmon Cakes

Salmon Chowder

Grilled Salmon Steaks

Poached Salmon

Poached Salmon in Halibut Aspic

Broiled Shrimp

Shrimp and Okra Stew

Broiled Rainbow Trout

Fried Rainbow Trout

Bean Cakes
Bean Mold
Boston Baked Beans
Green Beans with Fat Back
Green Pepper and Pink Bean Casserole
Dilled Wax Beans
Leather Britches Beans
Puyé Beans
Baked Beets
Skillet Cabbage
Baked Carrots
Boiled Corn Pudding
Corn Oysters
Fresh Corn Puffs
Parched Corn
Roasting Ears
Skillet Corn
Succotash
Baked Cucumbers
Fried Cucumbers
Baked Hominy
Fried Hominy
Jerusalem Artichokes Baked in Hot Ashes
Jerusalem Artichokes Sautéed in Oil and Vinegar
Baked Mushrooms
Baked Potatoes
Leeks and New Potatoes
Potatoes Baked in Hot Ashes
Potatoes Boiled in Broth
Baked Pumpkin
Baked Acorn Squash
Baked Butternut Squash
Boiled Butternut Squash
Baked Squash and Wild Onions
Baked Sweet Red Peppers and Yellow Squash
Baked Sweet Potatoes
Sweet Potato Cakes
Fried Green Tomatoes
Stewed Tomatoes
Baked Turnips
Baked Vegetables of the Vines
Baked Wild Rice and Carrots
Wild Rice

SALADS

Beet, Cucumber, and Onion Salad
Giant White Lima Bean Salad
Kidney Bean Salad
Pea Bean Salad
Cabbage Slaw
Cactus Salad
Marinated Cucumbers
Jerusalem Artichoke Salad
Mint Salad
Wilted Salad of Mustard Greens
Nasturtium Salad
Hearts of Palm Salad
Smothered Greens
Marinated Peppers
Wilted Spinach Salad
Hot Turnip Greens
Salad of Wild Greens

BREADS

Adobe Bread
Chippewa Bannock
Buckskin Bread
Carrot Bread
Golden Corn Bread
Corn Pone
Fried Gruel
Gruel
Hazelnut Cakes
Fried Hominy Grits

Hominy Grits
Indian Bread
Piñon Cakes
Popcorn
Squaw Bread
Sweet Potato Bread
Sunflower Seed Cakes
Tortillas
Wild Rice Johnny Cakes

SPREADS

Avocado Spread
Beach Plum Jam

Peach Honey

DESSERTS

Apples Roasted over Hot Coals
Applesauce
Hot Spiced Apricots
Berry Corn Cobbler
Blueberry Fritters
Cherries Simmered with Maple
    Sugar
Cranberry Fritters

Cranberry Sauce
Steamed Cranberry Pudding
Gooseberry Cobbler
Honey Tapioca Pudding
Indian Pudding
Maple-Sugared Nuts and
    Fruits
Venison Mincemeat

DESSERTS

Oranges Marinated in Honey
Roast Pineapple
Whipped Raspberries and
    Honey

Strawberries Poached in
    Honey Syrup

BEVERAGES

Apricot Drink
Honey Drink
Juniper Tea
Maple Drink

Mint Tea
Sassafras Tea
Yaupon Tea

INDEX

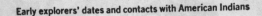
Early explorers' dates and contacts with American Indians

1. **VIKINGS 1000** landed south of Cape Cod
2. **COLUMBUS 1492** landed on San Salvador or Watling Island
3. **CABOT 1497** explored the coast of Maine
4. **PONCE DE LEON 1513** discovered and named Florida
5. **CORTEZ 1519** sailed from Cuba to Mexico
6. **VERRAZANO 1523** sailed along the eastern coast into Narragansett Bay
7. **BASQUES 1532** settled in Newfoundland
8. **CARTIER 1534** explored the Gulf of St. Lawrence
9. **CABEZA de VACA 1538** reached the Texas coast
10. **DE SOTO 1539** landed in Tampa Bay, Florida
11. **CABRILLO 1542** landed in Morro Bay, California
12. **MENÉNDEZ de AVILES 1565** founded the oldest city in the United States (St. Augustine, Florida)
13. **SIR FRANCIS DRAKE 1579** landed in Drakes Bay, California
14. **SIR WALTER RALEIGH 1585** attempted to settle Roanoke Island (the lost colony)

15. CHAMPLAIN 1604 explored from Acadia to New England
16. CAPTAIN JOHN SMITH 1607 settled in Jamestown, Virginia
17. JESUITS (FATHER LE JEUNE) 1632 settled along the
    St. Lawrence River
18. VÉRENDRYE 1738 settled in the area of the Dakotas
19. BEHRING 1741 explored the northwest coast
20. CAPTAIN COOK 1778 explored the northwest coast
21. LEWIS AND CLARK 1804 went across the continent from
    St. Louis to Fort Clatsop, Washington

Something special is cooking
at *Avon!*

A PINCH OF SOUL
by Pearl Bowser and Joan Eckstein

Hearty and elegant meals in a soul-food cookbook with a difference!　　　　　　　　**W227　$1.25**

CASSEROLE MAGIC
by Lousene Rousseau Brunner

Hundreds of simple and sumptuous one-dish meals!　　　　　　　　　　　**N341　95¢**

THE TONIGHT
OR NEVER COOKBOOK
by Virginia Graham

TV's favorite gal has gathered together the favorite recipes of her favorite gals—Lucille Ball, Leslie Uggams, Arlene Dahl, many more—in a cookbook that's fun to read and full of exciting dishes!

N280　95¢

ZEN MACROBIOTIC COOKING
by Michael Abehsera

A very special book offering an introduction to the ancient art of oriental cookery for longevity and rejuvenation!　　　　　　　　　　**W224　$1.25**

THE ART OF
AMERICAN INDIAN COOKING
by Yeffe Kimball and Jean Anderson

The foods of the rich American heritage, in recipes for the modern kitchen.　　　　　　　**N321　95¢**

THE COOK'S COMPANION
by Frieda Arkin

Indispensable—a dictionary and guidebook of essential culinary tips and terms—a companion to every cookbook!　　　　　　　　　　**V2358　75¢**

Wherever paperbacks are sold, or directly from the publisher. Include 10¢ per book for handling; allow three weeks for delivery. Avon Books, Mail Order Dep't., 250 W. 55th St., New York, N. Y. 10023